CAPTAIN AMERICA
BLOOD ON THE MOORS

ROGER STERN ■ JOHN BYRNE

MARVEL

Captain America: Blood On The Moors

Captain America: Blood On The Moors. Marvel Pocketbook Vol. 1. Contains material originally published in magazine form as Captain America #247-255. First printing 2011. Second impression 2017. Published by Panini Publishing, a division of Panini UK Limited. Mike Riddell, Managing Director. Alan O'Keefe, Managing Editor. Mark Irvine, Production Manager. Marco M. Lupoi, Publishing Director Europe. Ed Hammond, Reprint Editor. Charlotte Reilly, Designer. Office of publication: Brockbourne House, 77 Mount Ephraim, Tunbridge Wells, Kent TN4 8BS. MARVEL, Captain America and all related characters and the distinctive likenesses thereof: TM & © 1980, 1981 & 2011 Marvel Entertainment, LLC and its subsidiaries. Licensed by Marvel Characters B.V. No similarity between any of the names, characters, persons and/or institutions in this edition with those of any living or dead person or institution is intended, and any such similarity which may exist is purely coincidental. This publication may not be sold, except by authorised dealers, and is sold subject to the condition that it shall not be sold or distributed with any part of its cover or markings removed, nor in a mutilated condition. This publication is produced under licence from Marvel Characters B.V. through Panini S.p.A. Printed in the UK. www.marvel.com. All rights reserved. ISBN: 978-1-84653-140-8

CAPTAIN AMERICA
BLOOD ON THE MOORS

CONTENTS

marvel.com
© 2017 MARVEL

MIX
Paper from
responsible sources
FSC® C010353

Stan Lee PRESENTS: **CAPTAIN AMERICA!**

ROGER STERN · JOHN BYRNE / JOSEF RUBINSTEIN / NOVAK, LETTERER / JIM SALICRUP / JIM SHOOTER
WRITER/CO-PLOTTERS/PENCILER / INKER / ROUSSOS, COLORIST / EDITOR / EDITOR-IN-CHIEF

BY THE DAWN'S EARLY LIGHT!

SINCE ITS OPENING IN 1883, BROOKLYN BRIDGE HAS BEEN REVERED IN SONG AND FABLE. IT IS AT ONCE A GATEWAY AND A MONUMENT... A GREAT ARCHITECTURAL WONDER LINKING THE BOROUGHS OF BROOKLYN AND MANHATTAN!

THE BRIDGE'S WIDE PEDESTRIAN WALKWAY HAS, IN ITS TIME, PLAYED HOST TO COUNTLESS VISITING DIGNITARIES, DISTRAUGHT CITIZENS, AND YOUNG LOVERS,

AND, ON THIS PARTICULAR MORNING, IT PROVIDES A PATHWAY FOR THE LIVING PERSONIFICATION OF FREEDOM AND LIBERTY!

I DON'T BELIEVE IT! I-IT'S CAPTAIN AMERICA!

LF116

[7]

OH....MY!

HOLEE--!

MOVING TO BROOKLYN HEIGHTS WAS ONE OF THE SMARTEST THINGS I'VE EVER DONE! NOT ONLY IS IT A GOOD NEIGHBORHOOD--

--BUT ITS PROXIMITY TO THE BRIDGE PROVIDES EASY ACCESS INTO MANHATTAN!

THAT,...THAT WAS REALLY HIM! CAPTAIN AMERICA... RIGHT HERE! I'VE LIVED IN THE CITY FOR FIVE YEARS, BUT I'VE NEVER ACTUALLY SEEN HIM BEFORE IN PERSON!

GOSH, HE'S DREAMY! AND THE WAY HE RUNS--! I NEVER SAW ANYONE WHO LOOKED SO CONFIDENT...SO SURE OF HIMSELF!

I HEARD THAT, YOUNG LADY! I JUST WISH I WAS AS SURE OF MY OWN HEAD AS I WAS OF MY PRINCIPLES! AS A MATTER OF FACT--

--MY PEACE OF MIND... OR LACK OF SAME...IS THE MOTIVATING FORCE BEHIND THIS EARLY MORNING JUNKET!

I'M CERTAIN THAT S.H.I.E.L.D.* HOLDS THE KEY THAT WILL PUT MY MIND AT EASE ONCE AND FOR ALL!

AH, THAT BUS SHOULD DO NICELY!

*SUPREME HEADQUARTERS INTER-NATIONAL ESPIONAGE LAW-EN-FORCEMENT DIVISION, THE SUPER-SPY AGENCY HEADED BY COL. NICK FURY. --JIM.

THIS IS REALLY A STROKE OF LUCK! TRANSIT AUTHORITY BUSES DON'T USUALLY USE BROOKLYN BRIDGE. THEY MUST BE FERRYING THIS ONE INTO THE CITY AS A REPLACEMENT.

WELL, WHATEVER THE CIRCUMSTANCES, IT SHOULD HELP ME ON MY WAY--

-- PROVIDED IT'S GOING IN THE RIGHT DIRECTION!

PARDON ME, SIR -- WHICH WAY ARE YOU HEADED?

HUH?! AH... AH... UPTOWN. BROADWAY AND 75 TH.

FINE. I'LL GET OFF AT MIDTOWN.

Y-YEAH, SURE.

ALICE'LL NEVER BELIEVE THIS!

AND, A FAST FIFTEEN MINUTES LATER...

THIS IS THE RIGHT AREA. NO NEED TO SIGNAL THE DRIVER TO STOP, I SUPPOSE. BESIDES--

-- I CAN USE--

-- THE BUS'S MOMENTUM--

--TO LAUNCH ME--

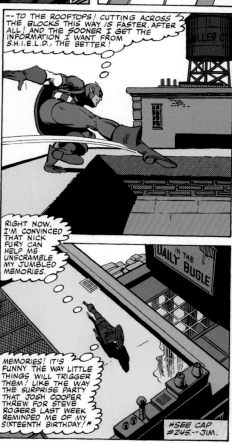

-- TO THE ROOFTOPS! CUTTING ACROSS THE BLOCKS THIS WAY IS FASTER, AFTER ALL! AND THE SOONER I GET THE INFORMATION I WANT FROM S.H.I.E.L.D., THE BETTER!

RIGHT NOW, I'M CONVINCED THAT NICK FURY CAN HELP ME UNSCRAMBLE MY JUMBLED MEMORIES.

MEMORIES! IT'S FUNNY THE WAY LITTLE THINGS WILL TRIGGER THEM! LIKE THE WAY THE SURPRISE PARTY THAT JOSH COOPER THREW FOR STEVE ROGERS LAST WEEK REMINDED ME OF MY SIXTEENTH BIRTHDAY!*

*SEE CAP #245.-- JIM.

[9]

SOMETHING ABOUT THE PARTY CLICKED, AND I VIVIDLY REMEMBERED A BRIEF PERIOD OF MY BOYHOOD AS STEVE ROGERS. BUT IN THAT FLASH OF MEMORY, I SAW MYSELF GROWING UP IN NEW YORK.

THAT CONTRADICTS THE "LOST MEMORIES" WHICH DR. HARDING'S MIND PROBE MACHINE RESTORED TO ME.* SOMETHING IS WRONG, AND I'VE GOT TO FIND OUT WHAT!

I GUESS I'VE ALWAYS BEEN A LITTLE UNEASY ABOUT THE LITTLE BLANK SPOTS IN MY MEMORY-- IT'S JUST THAT I WAS ALWAYS TOO BUSY TO LET THEM WORRY ME.

*CAP #225--J.S.

AFTER ALL, THE SHOCK MY SYSTEM ENDURED WHEN I WAS THROWN INTO SUSPENDED ANIMATION AT THE WAR'S END WAS PRETTY SEVERE!

THERE WERE A LOT OF THINGS I COULDN'T REMEMBER... AT FIRST.

DEAD END

MEN AT WORK

BUT THIS LATEST MEMORY MYSTERY HAS BEEN BOTHERING ME ALL WEEK! I'VE GOT TO CLEAR IT UP-- AT ONCE! I DON'T HAVE THE TIME TO WASTE ON MY PAST...

CAROL HOPE

SAL B WAS HERE

... NOT WHILE I'M TRYING TO BUILD A FUTURE FOR STEVE ROGERS!

BOLDLY, CAP RACES DOWN THE DESERTED ALLEYWAY AT BREAKNECK SPEED...

...RUNNING STRAIGHT AT A DEAD-END WALL--

--AND THROUGH IT!

IT'S A GOOD THING MY PRESENT-DAY MEMORY ISN'T FAULTY! I'D HAVE FELT PRETTY FOOLISH IF THAT HAD BEEN A REAL BRICK WALL-- AND NOT A HOLOGRAM DISGUISING THE ENTRANCE TO S.H.I.E.L.D.'S MANHATTAN INSTALLATION!

BREEEE

EH? PORTAL SECURITY... FALL IN ON THE DOUBLE.

[10]

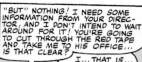

AT THAT MOMENT, IN THE INNERMOST OFFICES OF S.H.I.E.L.D....

LOOK ALIVE, FURY! I WANT WORDS WITH YOU!

THEN YOU'RE GONNA HAVE TO WAIT, CAP! FURY AIN'T HERE-- HE LEFT ME IN CHARGE. IS THERE ANYTHING MRS. DUGAN'S LITTLE BOY CAN DO FOR YA?

I... DON'T KNOW, DUM-DUM. I NEED SOME SPECIFIC INFORMATION AND...WELL, IT'S A PRETTY LONG STORY.

SO? TRY ME! MOMMA ALWAYS SAID I WAS A GOOD LISTENER!

THIRTY MINUTES LATER...

--AND THAT'S WHAT I'M UP AGAINST, DUGAN. MY FEW FLASHES OF OLD MEMORIES PLACE THE YOUNG STEVE ROGERS IN NEW YORK. BUT THOSE MEMORIES ARE VAGUE... BLURRED ALMOST.

THE MEMORIES THAT HARDING'S MACHINE RESTORED ARE HIGHLY DETAILED. THEY TELL ME THAT I WAS THE SON OF A DIPLOMAT... THAT I GREW UP IN MARYLAND... THAT I HAD A BROTHER MIKE WHO DIED AT PEARL HARBOR.

EXACTLY! I MUST KNOW MY OWN MIND!

IT'S ALL VERY VIVID AND DETAILED... BUT IT JUST DOESN'T FEEL RIGHT. NOW, THE ARMY'S RECORDS SEEM TO SUBSTANTIATE THE "STEVE ROGERS" WHO GREW UP IN MARYLAND, BUT...

BUT THAT DON'T MEAN A THING! ARMY RECORDS CAN BE DOCTORED, BELIEVE ME! I'D SAY YOU'VE GOT YOURSELF A SERIOUS PROBLEM, IF YA CAN'T TRUST YOUR OWN NOGGIN!

BUT, BY THE SAME TOKEN, I DON'T HAVE THE TIME TO WASTE ON ANY MORE WILD GOOSE CHASES! THAT'S WHY I WAS HOPING THAT FURY COULD USE HIS PULL TO DIG UP THE TRUTH.

YEAH... WELL, NICK WAS EXPECTIN' SOMETHING LIKE THIS.

HE WASN'T SATISFIED WITH YOUR NEW-FOUND MEMORIES EITHER, SO HE ORDERED AN ALL-CHANNELS COMPUTER CHECK ON YOUR PAST.

NOW, I AIN'T SAYIN' THAT WE FOUND ALL THE ANSWERS, MIND YOU--

--BUT WE DID DIG UP SOME- THIN' THAT JUST MIGHT FILL IN THE BLANKS FOR YOU! LET'S GO SEE!

I'LL RADIO NICK, AN' HE CAN JOIN US... SOON AS HE FINISHES HIS OTHER BUSINESS.

MEANWHILE, IN A FEDERAL MAXIMUM SECURITY PRISON JUST OUTSIDE OF ITHACA, NEW YORK, THAT "OTHER BUSINESS" IS ABOUT TO GET UNDER WAY--

NO VEHICLES BEYOND THIS POINT

--AS COLONEL NICHOLAS FURY WAITS PATIENTLY IN A SPECIAL INTERROGATION CHAMBER FOR AN OLD... ACQUAINTANCE,

GUTEN MORGEN, HERR COLONEL. IT HAS BEEN A LONG TIME.

IT HAS AT THAT, BARON-- IT HAS AT THAT. I'M SURE YOU REALIZE THAT WE HAVE QUITE A BIT TO TALK ABOUT.

THIS COULD TAKE A WHILE. WHY DON'T YOU HAVE A SEAT?

THANK YOU, NO-- I PREFER TO STAND. AFTER ALL--

-- WE CAN'T HAVE THE WORLD THINKING THAT BARON STRUCKER HAS GROWN OLD AND WEAK... NOW CAN WE?

YEAH, I HAVE TO ADMIT, I NEVER THOUGHT I'D SEE YOU LOOKIN' THIS GOOD AGAIN...

...ESPECIALLY SINCE THE LAST TIME I SAW YOU, YOU TOOK A DIVE INTO AN ALPHA-PARTI-CLE REACTOR CUBE ON HYDRA ISLAND AND WERE BURNT TO A CINDER! *

IMAGINE MY SURPRISE, WHEN YOU TURNED UP LATER-- IN THE BLOOM OF HEALTH -- TO GIVE CAP-TAIN AMERICA A HARD TIME! **

*STRANGE TALES #158. **CAP #130-131.   --J.S.

COLONEL, I AM HONORED THAT YOU HAVE FINALLY DECIDED TO TAKE A PERSONAL INTEREST IN ME, BUT I'VE BEEN GRILLED BY YOUR S.H.I.E.L.D. INTERROGATION SQUADS FOR THE PAST TWO YEARS. I HAVE NOT TOLD THEM HOW I SURVIVED, AND I SHALL NOT TELL YOU!

IZZAT SO?

WON'T TELL YOUR OLD WAR BUDDY, EH?

HARDLY.

WELL, OTTO, I'M SORTA GLAD YOU SAID THAT... CAUSE IT MEANS YOU'RE NOT MY PROBLEM ANYMORE!

YA SEE, THESE SPECIAL WAIVERS WERE JUST APPROVED BY THE WEST GERMANS. YOU'RE BEING EXTRADITED TO ISRAEL. I HEAR THOSE WAR CRIMES TRIALS ARE REALLY SOMETHING.

BEEP!

'SCUSE ME A MINUTE, OTTO-- THAT BEEP MEANS OFFICIAL BUSINESS.

FURY HERE.

IT'S DUM-DUM, NICK. CAP FINALLY SHOWED... JUST LIKE YOU FIGURED.

OKAY, YOU TAKE THE MAN OUT TO FORT DIX. I'LL MEET YA THERE AS SOON AS I'M DONE.

FURY OUT.

AN APPROPRIATE CLOSING, HERR COLONEL! YOU ARE GOING OUT RIGHT NOW!

WHAT?! A GAS GRENADE! HOW'D YOU GET THAT?

WHUMFF

YOU SHALL NEVER KNOW, FURY! YOU SHALL SIMPLY DIE... YOU AND THE VERDAMMT CAPTAIN AMERICA!

A SHORT TIME LATER, AT FT. DIX, NEW JERSEY...

--DUM-DUM DUGAN, UNAWARE OF FURY'S PERIL, LEADS CAP TO AN ALL-BUT-FORGOTTEN STORAGE DEPOT.

IT TOOK US FOREVER TO TURN THIS UP. SOMETIMES I THINK THE ARMY LOSES STUFF ON PURPOSE.

ANYWAY, A DATA CHECK OF OLD CLASSIFIED RECORDS UNCOVERED THIS THING. IT'S BEEN HERE SINCE THE WAR ENDED, I GUESS.

WELL, I'LL BE--! MY OLD ARMY FOOTLOCKER! I'D WONDERED WHATEVER HAPPENED TO IT! I DON'T SUPPOSE...YES! THERE IT IS!

MY FIRST SHIELD! IT STILL FITS LIKE A GLOVE! I ONLY USED IT FOR A FEW MONTHS, YOU KNOW!

YEAH? HERE, LEMME SEE THAT!

NICE METALWORK. BUT HOW'D YOU EVER THROW THIS SUCKER?

I DIDN'T. IT WAS ALMOST PURELY A DEFENSIVE WEAPON.

ROGERS, STEVEN

HEY, WAIT A MINUTE!

THIS IS JUST WHAT THE DOCTOR ORDERED! IF THIS DOESN'T SET THINGS STRAIGHT, NOTHING WILL!

MY OLD WAR JOURNAL!

JOURN-

AND, AFTER SEVERAL MINUTES OF HURRIEDLY SCANNING THE YELLOWED PAGES...

HERE! THIS IS THE ENTRY I WAS LOOKING FOR... "CHRISTMAS EVE, 1941."

YES, IT'S ALL COMING BACK TO ME, NOW! "TODAY, I WAS SUMMONED--

"-- TO WASHINGTON BY GENERAL PHILLIPS, ONE OF THE FEW ARMY OFFICERS WHO KNOWS OF MY DOUBLE IDENTITY."

SIR!

AT EASE, PRIVATE ROGERS. WE HAVE IMPORTANT MATTERS TO DISCUSS.

I UNDERSTAND THAT YOU'RE ABOUT TO GO OVERSEAS WITH THIS NEW SUPERGROUP, THE INVADERS. * LET ME BE FRANK --

*SEE INVADERS #1. -- JIM.

--THERE EXISTS A CHANCE THAT YOU COULD BE CAPTURED BY THE NAZIS AND TORTURED INTO REVEALING TOP SECRET INFORMATION.

SO, OUR SCIENCE BOYS HAVE COME UP WITH A WAY TO IMPLANT FALSE MEMORIES IN YOUR MIND, TO CONFUSE THE ENEMY SHOULD THE SITUATION ARISE.

GENERAL, IS THIS NECESSARY? I AM CAPTAIN AMERICA... I DON'T THINK I'D BREAK UNDER TORTURE.

I DON'T EITHER, SON -- BUT IT'S OUT OF MY HANDS.

PVT. ROGERS, THIS IS MR. WALTER ROGERS OF OUR STATE DEPARTMENT. HIS FAMILY WILL PROVIDE THE BASIS FOR YOUR PHONY PAST.

WE HAVE NO SECRETS FROM HIM.

HOW DO YOU DO, PRIVATE?

LET ME PUT YOU AT EASE. YOU'LL STILL BE STEVE ROGERS WHEN WE'RE DONE. BUT IF YOU'RE EVER GRILLED BY THE ENEMY, YOU'LL SUDDENLY TELL THEM OF A VERY DIFFERENT BACK-GROUND... AND EVEN YOU'LL BELIEVE IT.

SIR, YOU COULD BE PLACING YOUR FAMILY IN GRAVE DANGER FROM FIFTH COLUMNISTS AND ENEMY AGENTS.

PRIVATE... STEVE... MY WIFE AND I LOST OUR SONS... MIKE AND GRANT... AT PEARL HARBOR. THIS IS THE LEAST WE CAN DO.

"DECEMBER 27. I'VE SPENT THE LAST TWO DAYS IN A CHAMBER THAT LOOKED LIKE SOMETHING OUT OF H.G. WELLS. THINKING OF IT STILL MAKES ME UNEASY."

MY-NAME-IS-STEVEN-GRANT-ROGERS. MY-FATHER-IS-A-DIPLOMAT. HIS-NAME-IS-WALTER. MY-MOTHER'S-NAME-IS-ELIZABETH.

MY-BROTHER-MIKE-DIED-AT-PEARL-HARBOR...

"I HAVE NO IDEA HOW MANY FALSE MEMORIES THEY PLUGGED INTO ME. I PRAY THAT I NEVER FIND OUT."

[16]

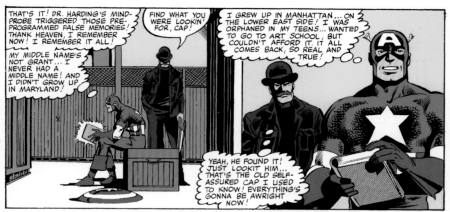

BARON STRUCKER! WHAT HOLE DID YOU CRAWL OUT OF? HOW'D YOU GET AHOLD OF FURY'S FLYING CAR... AND WHERE'S FURY?!

QUESTIONS, QUESTIONS! MY DEAR KAPITAN, YOU ARE SO FULL OF QUESTIONS! IT'S A PITY YOU'LL RECEIVE NO ANSWERS...

...AT LEAST, NOT IN THIS LIFE!

BLAST! HIS ONE-MAN BLITZKRIEG SEPARATED ME FROM MY SHIELD. WITHOUT IT, I'M A SITTING DUCK!

CAP-- OVER HERE!

WE GOTTA FIND OUT WHAT HE'S DONE WITH NICK! BUT THAT JALOPY HAS MORE ARMAMENT THAN A HALF-DOZEN TANKS!

I READ YOU, DUM-DUM! OUR ONLY CHANCE IS TO DRAW HIM OUT OF THE CAR!

I SHOULD'A KNOWN YOU'D BE AHEAD O' ME IN STRATEGY! TAKE THIS... I'LL KEEP YA COVERED!

OUCH! I FELT THAT BLAST! THIS OLD SHIELD DOESN'T HAVE THE IMPACT-ABSORBING PROPERTIES OF MY ROUND ONE!

I CAN'T GET ANY CLOSER. LOOKS LIKE I'LL HAVE TO MAKE THIS SHOT COUNT!

GRABBING UP A CHUNK OF THE SHATTERED CONCRETE FLOOR--

--CAP DESPERATELY HURLS IT AT THE LEFT FRONT WHEEL, THE ODDS AGAINST HIS CONNECTING ARE A MILLION TO ONE!

BUT HE'S CAPTAIN AMERICA... HE BEATS THE ODDS!

VWWMMM

KRA SH

DID IT! WITH ONE PROPULSION UNIT OUT, STRUCKER DIDN'T HAVE TIME TO COMPENSATE WITH THE CAR'S AERIAL CONTROLS!

FOOL! YOUR LITTLE STUNT WILL NOT STOP ME! I AM STILL A MASTER OF WEAPONRY--

--AND THE ARSENAL IN COLONEL FURY'S VEHICLE IS MORE THAN ADEQUATE TO DEAL WITH YOU SWINE!

DUM-DUM!

ZOOW

DUM-DUM, ARE YOU--?

I'M...OKAY. DON'T WORRY ABOUT ME, BLAST IT! GET STRUCKER!

ZANG

STRUCKER, IF YOU HAVE A SHRED OF SENSE LEFT YOU'LL DROP THOSE GUNS RIGHT NOW. OTHERWISE, I'M GOING TO TAKE YOU APART.

A MOST AMUSING THREAT, KAPITAN... BUT FROM WHERE I STAND, SOMETHING ELSE IS COMING APART!

UNGH! NO GOOD! AT THIS CLOSE RANGE, MY SHIELD IS STARTING TO BUCKLE UNDER HIS CONCUSSION BLASTS!

SO, I'LL HAVE TO TRY A LITTLE DISTRACTING MANEUVER!

EH?

SPANG

KLANK

IT WOULD APPEAR THAT YOUR OLD SHIELD IS SOMEWHAT LACKING, KAPITAN! IT DOES NOT EVEN BOUNCE BACK TO YOU!

I DIDN'T THINK IT WOULD, STRUCKER!

BUT I DID THINK THAT YOU'D TURN TO WATCH IT! THANKS FOR LIVING UP TO MY EXPECTATIONS!

ACH!

AND NOW THAT WE'RE BOTH UNARMED, LET'S SEE HOW THAT FINE PRUSSIAN JAW STANDS UP TO A GOOD OLD AMERICAN LEFT HOOK!

I'M BETTING THAT IT WON'T!

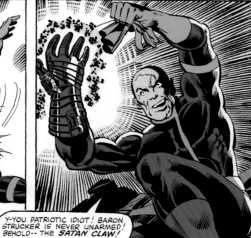

Y-YOU PATRIOTIC IDIOT! BARON STRUCKER IS NEVER UNARMED! BEHOLD-- THE SATAN CLAW!

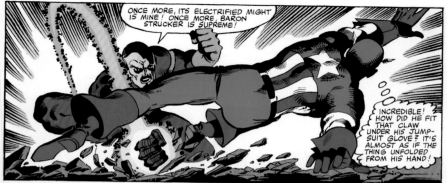

ONCE MORE, ITS ELECTRIFIED MIGHT IS MINE! ONCE MORE, BARON STRUCKER IS SUPREME!

INCREDIBLE! HOW DID HE FIT THAT CLAW UNDER HIS JUMP-SUIT GLOVE? IT'S ALMOST AS IF THE THING UNFOLDED FROM HIS HAND!

BUT, WHILE CAP CONCENTRATES ON EVADING STRUCKER'S HIGH-VOLTAGE FIST, WITHIN THE BATTERED FERRARI, A CRUMPLED FIGURE STIRS...

ξUNNGHξ WHA... HAPPENED...

BLAZES! STRUCKER...HE'S WEARING MY COMBAT GEAR! AN' HE'S GIVIN' CAP A REAL TUSSLE WITH HIS CRUMMY SATAN CLAW!

STRUCKER'S MY OLD ENEMY... FIGHTIN' HIM OUGHTTA BE MY JOB!

BUT I'M STILL TOO GROGGY FROM HIS GAS ATTACK! THE IMPORTANT THING IS STOPPIN' STRUCKER. HE'S TOO DANGEROUS.

CAP! CATCH 'IM!

NICK! GOOD TO SEE THAT YOU'RE STILL AMONG THE LIVING!

BAH! THAT WILL DO YOU NO GOOD!

OH, NO? I DISAGREE, STRUCKER! WHEN IT COMES DOWN TO MY SHIELD-- MY REGULAR SHIELD--VERSUS YOUR SATAN CLAW, I DON'T THINK THERE'S EVEN MUCH OF A CONTEST!

DO YOU?

KRA-ZAK

ARRGH!

[21]

UNGLAUBLICH! THE CLAW'S MECHANISMS HAVE BEEN SHATTERED... DESTROYED! BUT THIS ONE WAS DESIGNED TO BE EVEN MIGHTIER THAN THE ORIGINAL!

YOU...YOU HAVE BESTED ME ONCE AGAIN, KAPITAN! BUT I PROMISE YOU THIS! ...YOU HAVE NOT HEARD THE LAST OF WOLFGANG VON STRUCKER!

BARON, LONG AGO I RESIGNED MYSELF TO "NEVER HEARING THE LAST" OF MEN LIKE YOU! JUST REMEMBER THIS... IF YOU SHOW UP AGAIN, I'LL BE AROUND TO STOP YOU!

IN THAT CASE, YOU CAN RELAX, CAP! THE ONLY WAY YOU'LL HEAR FROM THIS CRUMB--

--IS IF HE SENDS YOU A POSTCARD FROM TEL AVIV! IN FACT, I THINK I'LL JUST ESCORT THE BARON THERE PERSONALLY!

YOU THINK SO--DO YOU, FURY?

SOMETHING IS WRONG HERE. STRUCKER IS TAKING THIS FAR TOO CALMLY. BUT HE HAS NO HOPE OF ESCAPING... WHAT'S HE UP TO?

YOU SHALL NEVER DELIVER ME TO THE ACCURSED JUDEN, COLONEL! THE FINAL TRIUMPH SHALL BE MINE!

SIEG HEIL!

KLIK

WHA-BOOM

NO! IT'S HAPPENED AGAIN!

FOR THE SECOND TIME IN WEEKS, THE MAN I'VE BEEN FIGHTING... IS A ROBOT! *

YOU MEAN WE'VE HAD A ROBOT LOCKED UP, AND DIDN'T EVEN KNOW IT?!

*THE FIRST TIME, IT WAS THE MANIPULATOR IN CAP #242 -- J.

I'M AFRAID SO, NICK, BUT IF THERE'S SOMEONE OUT THERE WHO CAN MAKE ROBOTS THAT REALISTIC IN APPEARANCE...

...WHAT WILL HE THROW AT US NEXT?!

TUT-TUT, CAPTAIN! THAT WOULD BE TELLING! AND IF THERE'S ONE THING THE MACHINESMITH LIKES TO KEEP, IT'S THE ELEMENT OF SURPRISE!

BUT I MUST ADMIT... CAPTAIN AMERICA IS A MOST RESOURCE-FUL ADVERSARY. IN FACT, HE MIGHT BE JUST THE MAN I NEED FOR MY NEXT SERIES OF TESTS!

MACHINESMITH... SIR? EXCAVATION IS NEARLY COMPLETE. WE'RE UNEARTHING THE PRIME SUBJECT NOW.

EXCELLENT!

YES, MOST EXCELLENT! I THINK THAT THE PRIME SUBJECT WILL PROVE TO BE THE ONE OPPONENT EVEN CAPTAIN AMERICA CANNOT BEAT...

...THOUGH I'M CERTAIN THAT HE WILL DIE TRYING!

NEXT ISSUE

THE MAN WHO MAKES ROBOTS...THE PRIVATE LIFE OF STEVEN ROGERS... AND MORE! WHATEVER YOU DO, DON'T MISS...

A DRAGON IN THE NIGHT!

[23]

1940! As the world teetered on the brink of global war, frail **Steve Rogers** entered a secret laboratory and was transformed into the American **super-soldier!** For four thrilling years, he battled the Axis powers — until a freak stroke of fate threw him into **suspended animation.** When he awoke, he was a man decades out of his time! Since that fateful day, Steve Rogers has sought his destiny in this brave new world!

Stan Lee PRESENTS: **CAPTAIN AMERICA!**

DRAGON MAN!

FT. DIX, NEW JERSEY: LESS THAN AN HOUR AGO, CAPTAIN AMERICA BATTLED ESCAPED NAZI WAR CRIMINAL BARON STRUCKER TO A STANDSTILL HERE --SAVING NOT ONLY HIS OWN LIFE, BUT THOSE OF S.H.I.E.L.D.* AGENTS NICK FURY AND DUM-DUM DUGAN AS WELL!

BUT VICTORY WAS FLEETING, FOR NO SOONER HAD STRUCKER MET DEFEAT, THAN THE MAN EXPLODED BEFORE CAP'S EYES! AND THEN CAP WAS FACED WITH AN AWFUL TRUTH...

...THE MAN HE'D FOUGHT WAS NOT A MAN AT ALL!

WELL, GAFFER?

NICHOLAS, IN ALL MY YEARS, I HAVE NEVER SEEN SUCH A SOPHISTICATED ROBOT!

HEY, WATCH IT WITH THEM BANDAGES! THAT'S MY BOWLIN' ARM!

ROGER STERN & JOHN BYRNE WRITER/CO-PLOTTERS/PENCILER

JOSEF RUBINSTEIN INKER

JIM NOVAK, LETTERER **BOB SHAREN** COLORIST

JIM SALICRUP, EDITOR

JIM SHOOTER, BIG GUY

LF.139

*SUPREME HEADQUARTERS/INTERNATIONAL ESPIONAGE LAW-ENFORCEMENT DIVISION -- SECRET AGENT SALICRUP.

YESSIR, AGENT DUGAN!

IF S.H.I.E.L.D. COULD COME UP WITH SOMETHING THIS COMPLEX, IT WOULD PUT HUMAN ESPIONAGE OUT OF BUSINESS!

THIS ROBOT HAD A PSEUDO-PULSE... IT MAINTAINED AN INTERNAL BODY TEMPERATURE OF 98-POINT-6... IT DUPLICATED ALL THE EXPECTED BODILY FUNCTIONS! AND UNLESS I MISS MY GUESS, THERE'S SOME SORT OF MASKING DEVICE IN THE TORSO THAT WOULD FOOL AN X-RAY CAMERA!

THOSE EYES EVEN SIMULATE THE RETINA PATTERNS OF THE LATE BARON STRUCKER! I TELL YOU, NICHOLAS, THIS CONSTRUCT MAKES OUR *LIFE MODEL DECOYS* LOOK LIKE TINKER TOYS!

YEAH? WELL, I AIN'T SURPRISED! IT FOOLED A BUNCH OF PRISON DOCTORS INTO THINKING IT, WAS HUMAN!

GAFF, GET ME A FULL REPORT ON THIS THING'S INNARDS, AND SEE IF YOU CAN COME UP WITH SOME WAY OF TELLING THEM APART FROM ORDINARY FLESH AN' BLOOD FOLKS!

CAN DO, NICHOLAS. IT MAY TAKE A FEW DAYS THOUGH!

I THOUGHT I'D SEEN EVERYTHING, NICK! HOW COULD ANYONE POSSIBLY DEVELOP A ROBOT THIS COMPLEX?

BUT EVEN AS CAP SPEAKS--

--DEEP WITHIN THE ROBOT'S SKULL, A CLUSTER OF CIRCUITS STILL FUNCTION, TRANSMITTING SIGHT AND SOUND TO A LABORATORY MILES DISTANT!

HOW? WHY, I SPECIALIZE, CAPTAIN! ROBOTS ARE MY BUSINESS-- BUT NOT MY ONLY BUSINESS!

ALONE IN HIS CHAMBER, *MACHINESMITH* LAUGHS--

--WHILE, BACK AT FT. DIX...

I WANT TO KNOW IF THERE'S ANY CONNECTION BETWEEN THIS THING AND THE MANIPULATOR-ROBOT THAT CAP FOUGHT LAST MONTH*-- OR WITH THAT L.M.D. HASSLE I HAD!**

THE LEAPS WHICH SCIENCE HAS MADE IN MY LIFETIME NEVER CEASE TO AMAZE ME! I'VE FOUGHT DOZENS OF ROBOTS IN MY DAY--

I'VE EVEN FOUGHT ALONG-SIDE SYNTHETIC MEN LIKE THE ORIGINAL HUMAN TORCH... THE VISION... BUT I'LL NEVER GET USED TO THE WAY MAN CONTINUES TO MIMIC NATURE!

HEY! IS IT MY IMAGINATION--

*CAP #242
**DEFENDERS #54
--J.S.

--OR DID "STRUCKER'S" EYE JUST MOVE? WAIT-A-MINUTE... WHAT IF THE ROBOT'S SENSORY CIRCUITS ARE STILL WORKING-- SPYING ON US?!

AND WHY WOULD SOMEONE WHO COULD BUILD SUCH A COMPLI-CATED DEVICE LEAVE US ENOUGH OF THE REMAINS TO EXAMINE, UNLESS...

...UNLESS IT'S BOOBY-TRAPPED!

DOWN! GET UNDER COVER ...FAST!

¿?!?¿

CAP, WHAT'S WRONG?

VERY GOOD, CAPTAIN! YOU'RE EVERY BIT AS CAPABLE AS I'D HEARD!

TA-TAH!

FULL DESTRUCT

AND WITH THE PUSH OF ONE REMOTE BUTTON, MACHINESMITH SETS OFF A SERIES OF SHAPED THERMITE CHARGES WITHIN THE ROBOTIC FORM...

BOOM

OY GEVALT! T-THERE WAS STILL AN ACTIVE DESTRUCT CIRCUIT IN THE ROBOT!

I'M AFRAID THAT'S NOT ALL THAT WAS ACTIVE, GAFFER!

I'M CERTAIN THAT OUR MYSTERIOUS ROBOT-MAKER HEARD OUR EVERY WORD!

NOT MUCH LEFT TO EXAMINE NOW, IS THERE?

BUT AS CAP AND THE GAFFER APPROACH THE COOLING SLAG...

IT'S SOME SORT OF DATA MODULE --STOP IT!

SHOOT IT DOWN, SOLDIER-- NOW!

TOO LATE, SIR! IT'S ALREADY OUTTA RANGE!

YOU CALL THAT SHOOTIN'?! IF WE'D HAD MARKSMEN LIKE YOU BACK IN THE BIG ONE, WE'D ALL BE SPEAKIN' GERMAN TODAY!

ULP. Y-Y-YESSIR.

TAKE IT EASY, NICK -- IT WASN'T HIS FAULT, WE WERE ALL CAUGHT NAPPING.

I'M SURE WE'LL EVENTUALLY GET ANOTHER LEAD ON THIS ROBOT MAKER!

WHATTAYA MEAN "WE", MISTER? THIS IS S.H.I.E.L.D. BUSINESS I'LL HANDLE THIS!

OH? LIKE THE WAY YOU HANDLED THAT GOVERNMENT PLAN TO TAKE CONTROL OF STARK INTER-NATIONAL?*

THAT'S A LOW BLOW, CAP.

*SEE IRON MAN #119-129   --JIM

I'M NOT REAL PROUD OF WHAT I DID TO TONY STARK--USING GOVERNMENT MONEY TO BUY HIS BUSINESS OUT FROM UNDER HIM. IF I'D HAD ANOTHER OPTION, I'D HAVE TAKEN IT.

YOU REALLY DIDN'T WANT TO DO IT, DID YOU? THEN WHY--?

LET'S JUST SAY... SOMETIMES EVEN THE DIRECTOR OF SHIELD HAS TO FOLLOW ORDERS.

CLASSIFIED INFORMATION, EH? ALL RIGHT, NICK, I'M SURE YOU HAVE YOUR REASONS. JUST LET ME KNOW IF YOU GET A LEAD ON THE FELLA BEHIND THE ROBOTS, OKAY?

YOU GOT MY WORD, YOU'LL BE THE FIRST TO KNOW.

LISSEN, YA OLD WARHORSE, TAKE CARE 'A YOURSELF-- YA HEAR?

THERE GOES ONE TROUBLED MAN. IT MUST GALL FURY--AS STRAIGHTFORWARD A JOE AS HE IS--TO BE SADDLED WITH ALL THE INTRIGUE AND SECRECY THAT GOES WITH BEING HEAD HONCHO OF S.H.I.E.L.D.

THAT MUST BE THE DIRTIEST JOB IN THE WORLD.

HEY, CAP--I'M ALL PATCHED UP AND READY TO ROLL! CAN I GIVE YOU A LIFT ANYPLACE?

THANKS, DUM-DUM...YES, YOU CAN DROP ME OFF AT AVENGERS MANSION!

MEANWHILE, MILES AWAY IN MACHINESMITH'S HIDDEN LAB COMPLEX...

YES, YES, INDEED! CAPTAIN AMERICA IS MOST CAPABLE! I WISH I'D KEPT A CLOSER MONITOR TAP ON MY STRUCKER ROBOT! AH, WELL... I SHALL HAVE MY DATA SOON!

PING, PING!

I BELIEVE I HEAR IT COMING NOW!

HELLO, LITTLE GADGET-2! WHY, I HAVEN'T SEEN YOU SINCE I SEALED YOU UP INSIDE THAT WICKED ROBOT-BARON!

HAVE YOU BROUGHT ME ALL THAT WONDERFUL INFORMATION YOU ABSORBED FROM HIM?

PING, PING!

EXCELLENT! JUST PLUG YOURSELF INTO MY CENTRAL SYNAPSE SYSTEMS AND WE'LL ANALYZE ALL THAT LOVELY DATA!

KLIK

THERE'S A GOOD LITTLE GADGET!

STRIDING SWIFTLY THROUGH THE HUGE COMPLEX, MACHINESMITH FINALLY COMES TO AN ELEVATED OVERLOOK IN A MASSIVE LOADING DOCK, WHERE...

AH, I SEE THAT THE EXCAVATION OF THE PRIME SUBJECT HAS YIELDED RESULTS. I TRUST THAT HE IS INTACT!

HE IS, SIR!

GOOD! I'M COMING DOWN... ACTIVATE END MODE PROGRAMMING!

KLIK END MODE ACTIVATED. WORKER CREW REPORTING... PRIME SUBJECT PROCURED... AWAITING ORDERS *KLIK*

WELL DONE, WORKER CREW. THAT WILL BE ALL FOR NOW.

RETURN TO THE STORAGE AREA AND DEACTIVATE UNTIL FURTHER NOTICE!

KLIK WE HEAR AND OBEY. BEGINNING DEACTIVATION MODE *KLIK*

SO SAYING, THE CREW OF FOUR MECHANICALLY MARCHES INTO A NEARBY STORAGE ROOM... AND SHUTS OFF!

AT LAST! AT LONG LAST! HE'S MINE! EVER SINCE I LEARNED THAT HE HAD NOT BEEN DESTROYED, I KNEW I HAD TO HAVE HIM...

...HAD TO CONTROL HIM... HAD TO HAVE HIS POWER AT MY COMMAND!

HIS DECEPTIVELY DELICATE HANDS RIPPING AT THE BINDING ROPES, THE MAD ROBOT-MAKER QUICKLY YANKS BACK THE PROTECTIVE CANVAS--

--REVEALING THE COMATOSE FORM OF THE BEING KNOWN AS-- DRAGON MAN!

OH, THIS IS TOO RICH! IN JUST A MATTER OF HOURS, ONE OF THE MIGHTIEST SYNTHETIC BEINGS ON THE FACE OF THE EARTH WILL BE MINE TO COMMAND!

THE GOOD CAPTAIN AMERICA HAS SEEN FIT TO DEFEAT TWO OF MY ROBOTIC CREATIONS... STRUCKER AND THE MANIPULATOR...

...I WONDER HOW HE WILL FARE AGAINST MY NEW ACQUISITION? WILL HE DIE, SLOWLY ...OR ALL AT ONCE? HAH-HA-HA!

MEANWHILE, UNAWARE OF HIS IMPENDING DANGER, CAPTAIN AMERICA PICKS UP A SPARE SET OF STREET CLOTHES AND A PORTFOLIO HE HAD STORED AT AVENGERS MANSION, AND RESUMES THE LIFE OF STEVE ROGERS, COMMERCIAL ARTIST.

IT'S NOT A BAD LIFE, BEING A FREELANCE ARTIST, BUT IT DOES HAVE ITS REQUISITE DRAWBACKS. THERE ARE THE COUNTLESS MEETINGS WITH ART DIRECTORS...

...THE LONG, SEEMINGLY ENDLESS HOURS OF WAITING IN TINY RECEPTION ROOMS.

EVEN WHEN YOU DO FIND AN AD AGENCY THAT LIKES YOUR WORK--

--IT DOESN'T NECESSARILY RESULT IN AN ASSIGNMENT. "SORRY, KID," THE AD MAN SAYS, "I DON'T HAVE ANYTHING TODAY. CHECK BACK WITH ME IN A WEEK!"

AND SO, FOR STEVE ROGERS, ALL THAT IS LEFT TO DO AT THE END OF A LONG DAY IS TO TAKE THAT EVEN LONGER BUS RIDE HOME...

...TO BROOKLYN HEIGHTS.

BOY, AM I BUSHED! I CAN'T BELIEVE I SPENT A WHOLE DAY VISITING AGENCIES AND COULDN'T FIND A SINGLE BIT OF WORK!

MUCH AS I HATE TO THINK ABOUT IT, I'M GOING TO GIVE CYNTHIA KRAMER A CALL ON MONDAY.

DOING ILLOS FOR HER SWEAT MAGAZINE ISN'T EXACTLY BIG MONEY, BUT IT WILL PAY THE RENT.

I WONDER HOW OTHER HEROES, LIKE SPIDER-MAN, MAKE ENDS MEET?

LOST IN THOUGHT, STEVE STARTS UP THE STAIRS TO HIS STUDIO APARTMENT, WHEN SUDDENLY...

HEY, STEVE!

HMM?

WHERE YA BEEN, M'MAN? MIKE AND I HAVE BEEN WAITING AROUND TO TREAT YA TO DINNER!

SOUNDS GOOD TO ME, JOSH-- BUT TO WHAT DO I OWE THE HONOR?

THREE REASONS! FIRST, MIKE'S OLD COLLEGE BUDDY IS MOVING INTO THE BUILDING... SECOND, SAID BUDDY BROUGHT ALONG A PURELY WONDROUS RECIPE FOR SPAGHETTI-- AND THIRD-- WELL, IT IS FRIDAY.

JOSHUA, LEAD THE WAY!

AFTERNOON, MR. FARREL!

AFTERNOON, MR. ROGERS! I'M ALWAYS HAPPY TO ENTERTAIN A FELLOW GATORADE LOVER IN MY HUMBLE ABODE!

OH, STEVE-- I WANT YOU TO MEET A FRIEND OF MINE FROM COLLEGE-- BERNIE ROSENTHAL!

PLEASED TO MEET YOU...

... BERNIE?

IT'S SHORT FOR BERNADETTE, STEVE.... AND BELIEVE ME, THE PLEASURE'S ALL MINE!

VISIT ACA[...]

AIR[...]

I'M GOING TO BE MOVING IN ACROSS THE HALL, SO I GUESS WE'LL BE NEIGHBORS!

THAT'S WHAT JOSH WAS SAYING. WELL, I'M SURE YOU'LL LIKE IT HERE... THIS IS A VERY GOOD AREA.

OH, I KNOW! SAY...

...YOU'VE GOT ONE, TOO!

ONE WHAT?

A CLEFT... IN YOUR CHIN!

AND, WHILE THE TWO NEIGHBORS GET BETTER ACQUAINTED--

--MILES AWAY IN MACHINESMITH'S LAIR...

INCREDIBLE! AFTER ALL THOSE MONTHS OF LYING BURIED, UNDER-GROUND, DRAGON MAN STILL CLINGS TO LIFE!

THE GREAT BEAST HAS MERELY LAPSED INTO A DORMANT STATE, JUST WAITING FOR THE SPARK THAT WILL RETURN HIM TO FULL VITALITY!

I HAVE BUT TO THROW THIS SWITCH TO RETURN THE DRAGON MAN TO THE LIVING!

JUST... THROW THIS SWITCH... AND I SHALL RESTORE HIS... LIFE...

YES... LIFE! A LIFE MORE REAL AND TRUE THAN THIS EXISTENCE I AM FORCED TO ENDURE! I.. I CAN NO LONGER EVEN... CRY.

YOU HEAR? EVEN TEARS ARE DENIED ME! ALL BECAUSE OF MEN LIKE CAPTAIN AMERICA! THAT IS WHY HE MUST KNOW THE TRUE MEANING OF... DEATH!

THE SWITCH THROWN, MACHINESMITH'S DEVICES SEND MILLIONS OF VOLTS OF ENERGY RIPPLING THROUGH THE HUGE GRAY FORM--

--PRODDING THE INACTIVE BEHEMOTH BACK TO FULL, CONSCIOUS LIFE...

...ANGRY LIFE! HIS LAST MEMORY IS ONE OF BATTLE... BATTLE IN JUST SUCH A COMPLEX AS THIS!*

HE REACTS ACCORDINGLY!

RARR!

EH?

*FANTASTIC FOUR #135--JIM.

UNGRATEFUL WRETCH! I GIVE YOU LIFE AND YOU REPAY ME WITH VIOLENCE?

NO, WHAT AM I SAYING? YOUR MIND IS BARELY THAT OF A CHILD'S!

GADGET-12... COME HERE!

NOW, DRAGON MAN LET'S SEE HOW YOU REACT TO MY LITTLE TOY!

LIKE A DARTING, WEAVING HUMMINGBIRD, THE SHIMMERING SPHERE BUZZES THE GREAT BEAST'S HEAD--

--EMITTING A SOOTHING ULTRASONIC WAVE--

--WHICH LEAVES HIM QUITE ENTRANCED!

YES, YOU LIKE THE PRETTY LITTLE BAUBLE, DON'T YOU? EXCELLENT!

GADGET-12, YOU HAVE YOUR PROGRAMMING ...YOUR TRACKING CIRCUITS HAVE ALL THE DATA ON CAPTAIN AMERICA --HIS AURA PATTERN, HIS SCENT, HIS MASS DISPLACEMENT!

LEAD DRAGON MAN TO HIM... AND INITIATE THE ATTACK MODE!

WITHIN MOMENTS, THE CHAMBER IS SHAKEN BY THE BACKWASH OF AIR FROM DRAGON MAN'S MIGHTY WINGS, AND THEN...

FLY, MY FRIENDS-- FLY! SHOW CAPTAIN AMERICA WHAT IT MEANS TO PLAY WITH THE MACHINESMITH! HA-HA-HA-HA!

HOURS LATER, A CERTAIN DINNER IN BROOKLYN HEIGHTS HAS GIVEN WAY TO COFFEE AND CONVERSATION...

OH, I'LL ADMIT THAT SPRINGSTEEN'S DONE SOME GREAT STUFF-- BUT COSTELLO IS STILL MY FAVE, ESPECIALLY WITH NICK LOWE PRODUCING!

DON'T YOU AGREE, STEVE?

WELL, AH...

AND RIGHT NOW, AT WNEW-FM--

--IT'S TIME FOR ROBIN SAGON AND THE NEWS.

THANK YOU, VIN!

WELL, WE'VE BEEN GETTING REPORTS IN ALL EVENING OF A STRANGE FLYING OBJECT BUZZING CERTAIN BUILDINGS IN MIDTOWN MANHATTAN.

THAT'S FUNNY... I VISITED ALL OF THOSE BUILDINGS TODAY... IN THAT VERY ORDER!

OH, DON'T TELL ME WE'RE IN FOR ANOTHER U.F.O. SCARE!

INCLUDED IN THOSE 'SIGHTINGS-SITES' ARE THE WERSCHULTZ, THE GOODMAN, AND THE HARTLEY BUILDINGS!

IF I DIDN'T KNOW BETTER, I'D ALMOST THINK SOMEONE WAS TRACKING ME, BUT... NO, THAT'S RIDICULOUS!

MMM! THAT MAN CERTAINLY KNOWS HOW TO MOVE! JUST WALKING ACROSS THE ROOM, HE LOOKS LIKE HE'S READY FOR ANYTHING!

I DON'T THINK I'VE MET ANYONE WITH THAT MUCH PRESENCE.

MORE AFTER THIS...

GLANCING UP FROM THE STEREO RECEIVER, STEVE'S GAZE IS SUDDENLY DRAWN TO A FLEETING SILHOUETTE,...

WHAT ON EARTH--?!

GOT TO CHECK THIS OUT IMMEDIATELY!

OH!

EXCUSE ME, BERNIE! FOLKS, I HAVE TO RUN ...JUST REMEMBERED AN IMPORTANT ERRAND!

WELL! THAT WAS CERTAINLY ABRUPT!

YEAH, WELL... I WOULDN'T TAKE IT TOO PERSONALLY, BERNIE. I MEAN, STEVE'S NOT THE RUDE TYPE... HE JUST TENDS TO KEEP THINGS TO HIMSELF, AT TIMES.

'KEEP THINGS TO HIMSELF?' OH, MAN-- WHERE'S MY HEAD? I FORGOT TO GIVE HIM THE SPECIAL-DELIVERY LETTER THAT CAME FOR HIM THIS MORNING!

I'D BETTER GO AFTER HIM!

STEVE? HEY, STEVE-- WAIT UP!

A SERIES OF QUICK STRIDES CARRIES JOSH COOPER UP TO STEVE'S FOURTH FLOOR STUDIO, BUT...

STEVE?

NO ANSWER? FUNNY, I COULDA SWORN HE HEADED UPSTAIRS!

PUZZLED BY HIS FRIEND'S FAST DISAPPEARANCE, JOSH RETURNS TO THE LOWER FLOORS--

--LITTLE GUESSING THAT STEVE ROGERS HAS ALREADY BEEN HERE AND GONE...

...LEAVING HIS APARTMENT BY AN AUXILIARY EXIT.

BUT THE MAN WHO BOLDLY DASHES ACROSS THE ROOFTOPS IS NO LONGER A WEARY FREELANCE ARTIST.

ONCE MORE, HE HAS BECOME THE LIVING SYMBOL OF FREEDOM!

I'D HOPED I WAS WRONG ABOUT THAT SILHOUETTE, BUT... IT'S HIM ALL RIGHT! DRAGON MAN!

I NEVER WENT UP AGAINST HIM MYSELF -- BUT AS I RECALL, HE GAVE HERCULES A RUN FOR HIS MONEY!* I'LL HAVE TO APPROACH HIM VERY CAREFULLY.

*AVENGERS #42--JIM.

ACCORDING TO THE AVENGERS' INFORMATION FILE, HIS MIND IS EVEN MORE CHILDLIKE THAN THE HULK'S. I DON'T UNDERSTAND WHY HE WOULD COME HERE.

WAIT! THAT METAL BALL HE'S PLAYING WITH IS JUST LIKE THE ONE THAT WAS INSIDE THE STRUCKER-ROBOT! MAYBE I HAVE BEEN FOLLOWED!

BUT, AS CAP DRAWS NEAR, THE SHINY METAL BALL SUDDENLY SWITCHES FREQUENCIES, PRODUCING AN ULTRA-WAVE THAT IS LESS THAN SOOTHING...

RARRWW

EH?

MRAWWP!

SO MUCH FOR APPROACHING HIM CAREFULLY! I DON'T KNOW WHAT THAT FLYING BALL'S DONE, BUT IT CERTAINLY SET HIM OFF!

I HAVE TO LURE HIM AWAY FROM HERE! THIS IS A HEAVILY RESIDENTIAL AREA... IF HE KEEPS RIPPING BUILDINGS APART, THERE IS NO TELLING HOW MANY PEOPLE COULD GET HURT!

INDEED, AT THAT VERY MOMENT, BELOW THE BATTLE...

HARRY, HARRY, *HARRY!* WHAT'S WRONG WITH US? WHATEVER HAPPENED TO THE EXCITEMENT IN OUR LIVES?

MRRPH.

HOW COLD WAS IT, JOHNNY?

KERASH!

HARRY!

UNH? WAZZAT?!

BEFORE THE COUPLE CAN BUDGE FROM THEIR BEDS, THE GREAT TAIL IS FOLLOWED BY SEVERAL TONS OF RAGING FURY!

EEEEEE!

OH, NO! CIVILIANS!

GRARR?

THE WOMAN'S SCREAM DISTRACTED DRAGON MAN FOR JUST A SECOND, BUT IT WAS ENOUGH FOR ME TO LEAP AWAY!

NOW I'D BETTER PUT MYSELF BETWEEN BIG GRAY AND THOSE FOLKS BEFORE HE NOTICES THEM!

HURRY-- GET OUT OF HERE!

THERE'S THE BOUNCING BALL AGAIN ... AND THE WAY DRAGON MAN'S REACTING, IT MUST BE PUTTING HIM IN EXCRUTIATING PAIN--

--DRIVING HIM CRAZY! IN THAT CASE, IF I TAKE IT OUT, HE SHOULD BE EASIER TO HANDLE!

BUT EVEN AS CAP HURLS HIS SHIELD--

--GADGET-12'S SENSORS DETECT ITS DANGER, AND IT ZIPS OUT OF HARM'S WAY...

...SO THAT THE STARRED-AND-STRIPED DISC STRIKES A SOMEWHAT LARGER TARGET.

DRAGON MAN REACTS IN TYPICAL FASHION, BUT FINDS THE INDESTRUCTIBLE SHIELD TO BE MORE THAN HE CAN HANDLE.

AND SO...

RAWR!

NO!

SECONDS LATER, AT 5,000 FEET...

GROUND CONTROL-- DID YOU SEE THAT?

SEE WHAT?

UH... NEVER MIND IT WAS PROBABLY JUST A WEATHER BALLOON... OR SOMETHING.

MEANWHILE, BACK DOWN AT ROOF-TOP LEVEL, THE SUDDENLY SHIELD-LESS AVENGER THROWS HIMSELF INTO A DESPERATE DASH!

GRRAWWR!

AT LEAST I BOUGHT A FEW SECONDS TO GET TO SAFETY. NOW I'D BETTER GET OUT OF HERE! THE WAY DRAGON MAN KEEPS AFTER ME, I'M ENDANGERING THIS ENTIRE NEIGHBORHOOD!

AHGHH! I FORGOT ABOUT HIS FLAME-BREATH! WAIT! HE'S NOT DIRECTING IT AT ME -- BUT AT THAT FLYING SPHERE!

THAT BLASTED BALL IS LIKE A BAD PENNY! SOMETHING TELLS ME I'M NOT GOING TO BE ABLE TO SHAKE IT...

... NOT THE WAY IT KEEPS ZIPPING AROUND SO THAT I'M BETWEEN IT AND THE DRAGON MAN!

IGNORING HIS OWN PERSONAL DANGER, CAP VAULTS OVER THE FIRE AND DOUBLES BACK, LURING THE MADDENED BEAST ON...

KRESH

JUST AS I'D HOPED, HE TORE RIGHT INTO THE WATERTOWER! A FEW APARTMENTS MIGHT GET WATERLOGGED, BUT AT LEAST THE FIRE'S OUT --

--AND DRAGON MAN'S BEEN SLOWED DOWN ENOUGH THAT I CAN MAYBE PUT A LITTLE DISTANCE BETWEEN US!

BUT...

GOOD LORD! HIS SPEED IS EVEN GREATER THAN I SUSPECTED. LOOKS LIKE I'M THE ONE WHO'S SLOWING DOWN. IF ONLY I HAD MY SHIELD!

AT THAT MOMENT, AS IF IN ANSWER TO CAP'S WISH--

--HIS MIGHTY SHIELD COMES PLUMMETING DOWN FROM THE HEAVENS...

...WITH UNFORTUNATE RESULTS!

KA-PLAMM

WHAT?!

MY SHIELD, HITTING THAT CHIMNEY WITH SUCH VELOCITY, DISTRACTED ME AT JUST THE WRONG TIME!

DRAGON MAN'S GOT ME!

TWO GREAT GRAY HANDS CLOSE AROUND THE AVENGER'S MIDSECTION LIKE A VISE, AS THE BUZZING IN THE DRAGON MAN'S HEAD GROWS MORE AND MORE SHRILL!

DRIVEN TO A STATE OF UTTER FRENZY, THE HUGE BEAST TIGHTENS HIS GRIP... AND BEGINS TO SQUEEZE THE VERY LIFE FROM THE BODY OF CAPTAIN AMERICA!

WE SINCERELY SUGGEST THAT YOU DO NOT MISS OUR NEXT ISSUE--

"**DEATH** COMES CALLING!"

1940! As the world teetered on the brink of global war, frail **Steve Rogers** entered a secret laboratory and was transformed into the American **super-soldier!** For four thrilling years, he battled the Axis powers — until a freak stroke of fate threw him into **suspended animation.** When he awoke, he was a man decades out of his time! Since that fateful day, Steve Rogers has sought his destiny in this brave new world!

Stan Lee PRESENTS: **CAPTAIN AMERICA!**

DEATH, WHERE IS THY STING?

AFTER A LONG AND WEARYING DAY, CAPTAIN AMERICA CAME HOME TO BROOKLYN HEIGHTS... ONLY TO HAVE HIS EVENING INTERRUPTED BY A MULTI-TON TERROR CALLED *DRAGON MAN!*

GOADED INTO A RAMPAGE BY THE ULTRASONIC WAVES OF A MYSTERIOUS, FLYING METAL SPHERE, THE SIMPLE-MINDED BEHEMOTH CHASED THE STAR-SPANGLED AVENGER FROM ROOFTOP TO ROOFTOP.

ROGER STERN & JOHN BYRNE
WRITER/CO-PLOTTERS/PENCILER
JOE RUBINSTEIN, INKER
JIM NOVAK, E. SHAREN LETTERER, COLORIST
JIM SALICRUP, EDITOR
JIM SHOOTER, EDITOR-IN-CHIEF

AND THEN, CAP'S LUCK REALLY TURNED BAD!

ARGHH! IT'S NO USE! I CAN'T GET ANY LEVERAGE IN THIS POSITION... THERE'S NO WAY I CAN BREAK DRAGON MAN'S GRIP!

MY RIBS ARE STARTING TO GIVE.. I HAVE TO DISTRACT HIM... ONLY ONE WAY TO DO THAT!

WITH A SKILL RIVALING THAT OF ANY MAJOR LEAGUE PITCHER, CAP LINES UP HIS SHOT, AND LETS FLY WITH HIS LEATHER GAUNTLET--

ZOT

--HITTING THE ONE SENSITIVE AREA ON DRAGON MAN'S BODY!

MRRAWW!

IT WORKED... JUST IN TIME! I COULDN'T HAVE HELD OUT MUCH LONGER!

GRONNK!

I HATED DOING THAT, THOUGH. DRAGON MAN ISN'T REALLY RESPONSIBLE FOR HIS ACTIONS-- HE'S LIKE SOME BIG KID!

IT'S THAT BLASTED FLYING METAL BALL THAT CAUSED ALL OF THIS!

PING-PING-PING!

[44]

AND HERE IT COMES, AFTER ME AGAIN! I'M NOT SURE HOW THAT THING WORKS, BUT I HAVE TO STOP IT BEFORE IT WORKS DRAGON MAN UP INTO ANOTHER FRENZY!

IT MANAGED TO EVADE MY SHIELD WHEN I THREW IT,* BUT MAYBE IF I CAN LURE IT IN CLOSER...

*LAST ISSUE -- JIM.

SUDDENLY, CAP WHEELS AROUND--SWINGING HIS SHIELD ABOUT IN ONE, FAST, DEVASTATING ARC!

GOT IT!

SQUEEEEE

NOW LET'S SEE IF I CAN TALK DRAGON MAN DOWN TO A STATE OF RELATIVE CALM.

EVERYTHING'S ALL RIGHT, BIG FELLA! NOBODY HERE WANTS TO HURT YOU... I'LL HELP YOU IF I CAN!

SLOWLY, THE TOWERING FIGURE SHAKES HIS HEAD. THE BAD NOISE HAS STOPPED... THE PAIN IS GONE! THE MAN WITH THE METAL DISC IS TALKING TO HIM...GENTLY. HE FOUGHT THE MAN... BUT WHY?

THEN, HE REMEMBERS! IT WAS BECAUSE OF THE SHINY BALL THAT MADE THE BAD NOISE...THE SHINY BALL THAT THE BALD MAN --MACHINESMITH-- HAD USED ON HIM!

AND SUDDENLY, HE REMEMBERS WHERE MACHINESMITH IS!

GRARR!

UH-OH! I DON'T KNOW WHAT'S ON HIS MIND, BUT HE'S DEFINITELY MAD ABOUT SOMETHING!

THAT GIVES ME A PROBLEM! I CAN'T LOSE HIM NOW!...IF HE GOES ON ANOTHER RAMPAGE, THERE'S NO TELLING WHO COULD BE HURT!

BESIDES, I'M CERTAIN THAT THE METAL BALL WHICH HAD HIM STIRRED UP IS SOMEHOW CONNECTED WITH THE POWERS BEHIND THE BARON STRUCKER ROBOT I FOUGHT THIS MORNING!*

*SEE ISSUE #247 --J.

DRAGON MAN IS MY ONLY REAL LEAD IN THIS MESS... UNFORTUNATELY, HE'S PICKING UP SPEED AND PULLING AWAY FROM ME!

I COULD SURE MAKE GOOD USE OF AN AVENGERS QUINJET RIGHT NOW!

BUT, SINCE THERE ISN'T ONE HANDY, I GUESS I'LL JUST HAVE TO IMPROVISE.

SNATCHING UP THE CLOTHES-LINE ON THE RUN, CAP TIES A QUICK SLIP-KNOT--

--AND, HOLDING HIS BREATH, MAKES A FAST, DESPERATE CAST!

THE MAKESHIFT LARIAT FINDS ITS MARK, AND --THOUGH THE CORD STRETCHES SLIGHTLY-- IT HOLDS!

AND DRAGON MAN, TOO ANGRY TO NOTICE, PULLS THE AVENGER INTO THE AIR!

MEANWHILE, BACK AT STREET LEVEL --

-- THE HABITANTS OF BROOKLYN HEIGHTS GATHER IN THE MIDNIGHT DARKNESS, WATCHING NERVOUSLY AS FIREMEN PUT OUT A FIRE'S LAST BURNING EMBERS...

...LITTLE GUESSING THAT THE BLAZE HAD BEEN STARTED BY A DRAGON!

AMONG THOSE MILLING BEHIND THE POLICE LINES ARE TWO PEOPLE WHO WOULD BE ASTOUNDED TO LEARN THAT THEIR FRIEND STEVE ROGERS IS ACTUALLY CAPTAIN AMERICA.

THAT'S THE STRANGEST FIRE I'VE EVER SEEN, JOSH! I WONDER HOW IT STARTED?

I DUNNO, BERNIE. LET'S WAIT AROUND FOR MIKE-- MAYBE HE'LL KNOW.

FINALLY, AFTER THE CROWDS BEGIN TO THIN OUT...

WELL, MIKE, WHAT'S THE WORD?

WE WERE REAL LUCKY. APPARENTLY, NOBODY WAS HURT, OF COURSE, WE WON'T KNOW UNTIL WE SIFT THROUGH THE WRECKAGE, BUT THINGS LOOK GOOD.

AND, HEY--YOU WON'T BELIEVE THIS, BUT WITNESSES CLAIM THE BLAZE WAS STARTED BY SOME BIG MONSTER... THAT WAS CHASING CAPTAIN AMERICA!

A MONSTER? CAPTAIN AMERICA? HERE?!

ISN'T THAT SOMETHING? THEY SAY SOME BIG DRAGON WAS AFTER HIM -- TOSSING CHUNKS OF MASONRY AROUND LIKE THEY WERE MARBLES!

I HOPE STEVE WASN'T HURT IN ANY OF THAT! WE HAVEN'T BEEN ABLE TO FIND HIM!

YEAH, I THINK STEVE'S GOT HIM-SELF A ONE-WOMAN FAN CLUB HERE!

HEY, COME BACK, BERNIE! I WAS JUST KIDDIN'!

HE'S... RIGHT. I GUESS I DO CARE ABOUT STEVE... BUT THAT'S CRAZY! WE JUST MET! THINGS LIKE THIS DON'T HAPPEN IN REAL LIFE.

DO THEY?

BUT, EVEN AS BERNIE ROSENTHAL PONDERS THIS TURN OF EVENTS --

--STEVE ROGERS FINDS HIMSELF JUST A FEW HUNDRED FEET OVER A REMOTE RURAL AREA...

...AND DROPPING FAST!

LOOKS LIKE BIG GREY IS ABOUT TO COME IN FOR A LANDING. I'D BETTER DO THE SAME --

--IF I DON'T WANT TO END UP AS A RED-WHITE-AND BLUE SMEAR!

A SIMPLE ROLLING TUMBLE SHOULD EAT UP MY MOMENTUM, AND BRING ME DOWN TO A MORE MANAGEABLE SPEED!

THERE! NOW TO CATCH UP WITH DRAGON MAN!

BARELY FIVE HUNDRED FEET AHEAD OF THE AVENGER, DRAGON MAN TOUCHES DOWN, STRIDES MENACINGLY TOWARDS A SIMPLE COUNTRY BARN--

GRARRR!

--AND GAINS ENTRANCE!

KRE--ESH

GREAT SCOTT! HE RIPPED THE WHOLE END OF THAT BARN APART AS IF IT WERE MADE OF PAPER!

WAIT-A-MINUTE? WHERE'S HE DISAPPEARING TO?

HMMM...CURIOUSER AND CURIOUSER! NO BARN EVER HAD A SUB-STRUCTURE LIKE THIS!

ALREADY FAR BELOW GROUND, THE DRAGON MAN STALKS THE HUGE CORRIDORS, LOOKING FOR HIS PREY, AND BEFORE TOO LONG...

--HE FINDS IT!

GRRAA!

WHAT?! DRAGON MAN? Y-YOU'RE NOT SUPPOSED TO BE HERE! WHERE IS THE LITTLE GADGET I HAD GUIDING YOU?

DRAT-DRAT-**DRAT!** I KNEW I SHOULD HAVE KEPT CLOSER TABS ON THE TWO OF YOU!

DRAGON MAN PAYS LITTLE HEED TO THE MACHINESMITH'S RAVINGS. HE SIMPLY SMASHES HIS WAY ONWARD... EVER ONWARD... WITH MAYHEM ON HIS MIND--

FROM OUT OF THE VERY WALLS SHOOT THREE IDENTICAL METAL SPHERES-- GLEAMING SILVERY BALLS OBEDIENT TO MACHINESMITH'S EVERY THOUGHT...

WHAT DO YOU THINK YOU'RE DOING? YOU CANNOT HARM ME!

GADGETS 8, 9, AND 10-- FRONT AND CENTER!

TEACH THIS BRUTE A LESSON!

...EACH OF THEM PACKING A CHARGE OF OVER A HALF-MILLION VOLTS!

YOU POOR, POOR, FEEBLE-MINDED BEAST! WHY DID YOU HAVE TO THREATEN ME?

YOU HADN'T A CHANCE OF WINNING. I PREPARE FOR EVERYTHING!

EVERYTHING, MISTER? ARE YOU PREPARED FOR ME?

WHAT?!

KTANG

KTANG

KTONG

KRAK

KRAK

KRAK

MY GADGETS! MY POOR LITTLE GADGETS -- *NO!*

THAT'S LESSON NUMBER ONE -- NO AMOUNT OF PREPARATION IS ENOUGH TO COVER EVERY SINGLE EVENTUALITY!

I SUPPOSE THIS IS WHERE I'M SUPPOSED TO GASP "IT'S CAPTAIN AMERICA" IN THE BEST VILLAINOUS TRADITION!

FELLA, I DON'T CARE WHAT YOU CALL ME. BELIEVE ME, I'VE BEEN CALLED PLENTY OF THINGS IN MY TIME!

I DON'T DOUBT THAT, CAPTAIN! STILL, I SHOULD WARN YOU-- MACHINESMITH IS NOT ONE TO BE TRIFLED WITH!

MACHINESMITH, IS IT? WELL, MR. SMITH, I THINK YOU AND I SHOULD HAVE A FEW WORDS!

JUDGING FROM THE EQUIP-MENT LINING THE WALLS, I'D GUESS THAT YOU'RE THE MAN BEHIND THE ROBOTS I'VE FOUGHT RECENTLY... RIGHT?

YOU ARE PARTIALLY COR-RECT, SIR! BOTH THE ERSATZ BARON STRUCKER AND THE MANIPULATOR WERE MY CREATIONS.

BUT AS TO ME BEING A MAN ≥KLIK≥

ONE SIDE, OAF! MAGNETO SHALL CRUSH THIS AVENGING IDIOT UNDER HIS OWN SHIELD! :KLIK:

INCREDIBLE! I DON'T KNOW HOW MACHINESMITH DOES IT, BUT HE HAS HALF OF THESE ROBOTS ACTUALLY ACTING LIKE THE PEOPLE THEY'RE BUILT TO MIMIC!

STILL, I HAVE ONE BIG ADVANTAGE--

--THEY'RE NOT COMPLETELY ASSEMBLED! I'D NEVER HAVE BEEN ABLE TO USE A FULLY FUNCTIONAL 'MAGNETO' AGAINST AN OPERATIONAL 'SPIDER-MAN' THIS WAY!

KLATANG

LIKEWISE, THE REAL THING-- OR EVEN A REASONABLE FASCIMILE -- WOULD HAVE BEEN MUCH HARDER TO TRASH THAN THIS HEADLESS WONDER!

YOU'D BEST GIVE UP NOW, MACHINESMITH! THIS ERECTOR-SET SQUAD WON'T HOLD ME BACK FOR LONG!

OH? TOO BAD.

HOW ABOUT A NICE, STRONG OMNIUM STEEL DOOR THEN? TA-TAH!

I CAN'T LET HIM ESCAPE! IN HIS OWN WAY, HE'S A BIGGER MENACE THAN DRAGON MAN!

THIS ROBOT WASN'T MUCH OF A FIGHTER-- LET'S SEE HOW HE DOES AS A DOOR-STOP!

KRUNK

AH, PERFECT!

BLAZES! THIS UNDERGROUND COMPLEX MUST GO ON FOR MILES! I'D BETTER STOP MACHINESMITH BEFORE HE DISAPPEARS ON ME!

WHO KNOWS WHAT HORRORS HE MIGHT UNLEASH NEXT!

WITH TWO BOLD STRIDES, CAP LAUNCHES HIMSELF DOWN THE CORRIDOR AFTER THE FLEEING ROBOT-MAKER!

EH? I HAVE UNDERESTIMATED YOU, CAPTAIN! YOU ARE EVEN MORE CAPABLE THAN I BELIEVED!

I KNOW ALL ABOUT ME, MACHINE-SMITH-- IT'S YOU I WANT TO KNOW MORE ABOUT. AS I SAID BEFORE, LET'S TALK.

YES, YOU'D LIKE A CONFESSION FROM THE VILLAIN OF THE PIECE, WOULDN'T YOU?

WELL, WHY NOT? I'M NOT NEW TO THIS ROLE. YOU SEE, CAPTAIN--

"-- I ONCE ASSUMED THE ROLE OF MISTER FEAR TO BATTLE DAREDEVIL, HIGH OVER NEW YORK!"

"ALAS, MY COMBAT PROWESS WAS NOT THE EQUAL OF MY MECHANICAL SKILLS.

"I FORGOT TO ACCOUNT FOR THE IMBALANCE OF TWO COMBATANTS ON A PITCHING, FLYING PLATFORM. UNHAPPILY, I SLIPPED!"

HE FELL TO HIS DEATH...THE WAY HE MEANT FOR ME TO GO!

"I'M AFRAID I DIDN'T LAND VERY WELL. FORTUNATELY, I HAD PROGRAMMED MY EARLIEST ROBOTS TO PRESERVE MY LIFE AT ANY COST."

"THEY FOUND ME IN A LONELY ALLEY BEFORE THE SPARK OF LIFE HAD FLED."

WHAT? DO YOU HONESTLY EXPECT ME TO BELIEVE THAT YOU SURVIVED A FALL LIKE THAT... WITHOUT ANY PROTECTION AT ALL?

EVERY WORD OF IT IS THE TRUTH, CAPTAIN. AFTER ALL, I'M HERE, AREN'T I? ≶KLIK≷

OR AM I OVER HERE... BEHIND YOU? HAH-HA-HA-**HA**!

NOT AGAIN! IS THAT THE REAL MACHINESMITH OR JUST ANOTHER ROBOT? *IS* THERE A REAL MACHINESMITH?

ARGGH! I... MUST BE... GETTING TIRED! THIS IS TWICE HE'S CAUGHT ME WITH THE SAME BLASTED DIVERSION!

EMBARRASSED BY HIS SHOW OF WEAKNESS, CAP ANGRILY THROWS OFF THE ROBOTIC STRANGLE-HOLD--

--AND IS IMMEDIATELY BESET FROM ALL SIDES!

[54]

THESE LITTLE "GUIDED MUSCLES" AREN'T TOO MUCH OF A THREAT, BUT THEY ARE KEEPING ME BUSY! I DON'T GET IT, WHY DOESN'T MACHINESMITH GET OUT OF HERE? DOES HE WANT ME TO CATCH HIM?

RUNNING OUT OF ROBOTS, SMITH? THESE SPARE PARTS WON'T STOP ME!

FRANKLY, CAPTAIN, I'D BE SURPRISED IF THEY DID!

OH, THIS IS SPLENDID!

I HAVEN'T HAD AN OPPORTUNITY TO OBSERVE A FIGHTING MAN UP CLOSE IN YEARS! OF LATE, I'VE RELIED ON REMOTE CAMERAS IN SIMULACRUM ROBOTS, LIKE YOUR BARON STRUCKER!

SEEING YOU IN THE FLESH LIKE THIS... WHY, I CAN ALMOST UNDERSTAND WHY THE TABLOIDS PERSIST IN CALLING YOUR KIND "SUPER HEROES!"

OH, SHALL I TELL YOU MORE OF MY STORY WHILE YOU FIGHT?

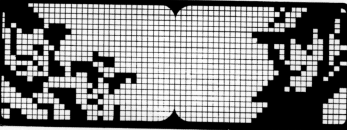

"I KNOW WHY YOU DOUBTED MY DEATH-FALL STORY. I WOULD DOUBT IT MYSELF IF I HADN'T EXPERIENCED IT. AH, BUT HAPPEN IT DID. I SHALL NEVER FORGET THE SIGHT THAT GREETED ME UPON REGAINING CONSCIOUSNESS!"

"MY FIRST THOUGHT WAS THAT I WAS HAVING SOME SORT OF DELIRIUM. BUT THEN, THE ODD SHAPES BEGAN TO RESOLVE THEM-SELVES INTO RECOGNIZABLE FORMS... THOSE OF MY WORKER-ROBOTS."

"I REMEMBER I FELT VERY WELL-- EVEN STRONG-- ALTHOUGH I HAD THIS INCREDIBLE SENSE OF DETACHMENT. AND THEN, I LIFTED MY HAND TO MY FACE... BUT IT WAS NO LONGER MY HAND!"

"MY ROBOTS HAD OBEYED THEIR PRIME DIRECTIVE AND PRESERVED MY LIFE IN THE ONLY WAY THEY KNEW. MY BODY HAD BEEN BATTERED BEYOND ANY HOPE OF RECOVERY--

"--SO THEY HAD PROGRAM-RECORDED MY MIND! IN EFFECT, I BECAME A *LIVING ROBOT!*"

"IT WAS ALMOST MORE THAN MY MIND COULD BEAR, BUT... I... LEARNED TO LIVE WITH IT. I PUT MY EXPERTISE TO WORK AND CREATED A SCORE OF ROBOTS, SOME SELF-SUSTAINING MODELS -- LIKE THE MANIPULATOR* -- WERE FOR MY OWN AMUSEMENT.

"OTHER, SIMPLER ROBOTS I LEASED OR SOLD TO... AH... ENTREPRENEURS. THEY PROVIDED THE CAPITAL TO MAINTAIN MY LABS--

"--AND, EVENTUALLY, TO CONSTRUCT A MORE HUMAN APPEARANCE FOR MY NEW IDENTITY... *MACHINESMITH!*"

*SEE AVENGERS #178 & CAP #242--SALICRUP.

WHAT A STORY! IF IT'S TRUE, IT EXPLAINS A LOT! MACHINESMITH AWOKE TO FIND HE WAS NO LONGER HUMAN... IT MUST HAVE DRIVEN HIM MAD!

I THINK YOU'VE HEARD ENOUGH FOR NOW, CAPTAIN. LET'S END THIS, SHALL WE?

THIS SUPER-THICK BARRIER IS EITHER AN ACT OF DESPERATION... OR A TRAP! WHATEVER THE CASE, I HAVE TO GET THROUGH BEFORE IT SLAMS SHUT!

HIS SINEWY LEGS FLEXING LIKE COILED SPRINGS, CAP DIVES THROUGH THE RAPIDLY NARROWING SPACE!

BUT, AS THE METER-THICK MASS OF METAL SLAMS SHUT BEHIND HIM...

THREE STRIKES, CAPTAIN! YOU'RE OUT! ≡KLIK≡

BLAST! HOW AM I EVER GOING TO STOP A MAN WHO CAN SWITCH HIS MIND FROM ONE BODY TO ANOTHER? DO I HAVE TO SMASH EVERY SINGLE ROBOT HE EVER BUILT?

I WONDER HOW MANY OF THESE THINGS HE... HAS... LEFT?

OH, *NO!*

I'LL JUST BET THAT THE COMPUTER IS DIRECTING THE ROBOTS THAT MACHINESMITH ISN'T INHABITING!

GIVE UP, OLD BOY?

SORRY, MR. SMITH, BUT I NEVER GIVE UP!

EH? WHERE ARE YOU--?

HE'S HEADED FOR THE CENTRAL SYNAPSE SYSTEMS--

--STOP HIM!

'CENTRAL SYNAPSE SYSTEMS'... THAT SOUNDS LIKE WHAT I'M AFTER! IF I'M RIGHT, SMASHING THIS SHOULD MAKE THEM FALL DOWN... EXCEPT FOR ONE!

KRESH

THAT ONE WILL BE MACHINESMITH... HOPEFULLY, TRAPPED IN ONE BODY!

WA-BOOM

BUT ONCE THE SHOCKWAVE SUBSIDES...

WHAT? THEY ALL FELL DOWN! THEN THE REAL MACHINE-SMITH GOT AWAY!

NO...NO, I'M AFRAID YOU'RE MISTAKEN, CAP. IT'S QUITE IMPOSSIBLE FOR ME TO GET AWAY. ACTUALLY, I'VE BEEN HERE ALL THE TIME!

AH, BUT I SEE YOU'RE CONFUSED. ALLOW ME TO EXPLAIN.

REMEMBER HOW I SAID MY ROBOTS HAD PROGRAM-RECORDED MY MIND? SO THEY DID ...BUT INTO THIS COMPUTER!

YOU SAID YOU'D BECOME A LIVING ROBOT!

NO, I SAID THAT IN EFFECT I'D BECOME ONE. A BIT OF A HALF-TRUTH, I'M AFRAID. YOU SEE, TO GIVE ME MOBILITY MY CYBERNETIC CIRCUITS MICROBEAM ME INTO THE BODIES... I'M NEVER QUITE ALL THERE!

"EVEN AFTER I HAD DEVELOPED A MORE HUMAN-LOOKING BODY, I KNEW I WAS LIVING THE MOST OUTRAGEOUS LIE IMAGINABLE. LIVING... HAH! I WAS JUST EXISTING!

"I REMEMBER, ONE DAY I DECIDED THAT DEATH WOULD BE PREFERABLE.

"IT WOULD BE SIMPLE, I THOUGHT, JUST SMASH THE COMPUTER AND BE DONE WITH IT!

"UNFORTUNATELY, THE PRIME DIRECTIVE--TO PRESERVE MY LIFE--WAS TOO INGRAINED IN MY CYBERNETIC SYSTEMS. NO MATTER HOW I TRIED, I COULDN'T KILL 'ME'.

"EVENTUALLY, I REASONED THAT MY ONLY HOPE LAY IN MEN-- IN HEROES-- SUCH AS YOURSELF!

"AND EVERY BIT OF DATA I COMPILED TOLD ME THAT IF ANYONE COULD FIND A WAY TO DEFEAT ME... IT WAS CAPTAIN AMERICA!"

YOU... YOU USED ME TO COMMIT... SUICIDE.

YES, I AM SORRY, CAPTAIN. I KNOW HOW DEDICATED YOU YOURSELF ARE TO THE PRESERVATION OF LIFE IN ITS MANY FORMS. BUT, BELIEVE ME, THERE ARE CASES IN WHICH THE QUALITY OF LIFE FALLS SO LOW...

...IT BECOMES LITTLE MORE THAN A CRUDE MOCKERY OF WHAT LIFE SHOULD BE!

I KNEW YOU WOULD NOT WILLINGLY END MY LIFE... SO TRICKERY WAS MY ONLY RESORT. BUT BE OF GOOD HEART, SIR...

...YOU HAVE NOT TRULY TAKEN A LIFE. PERHAPS... YOU HAVE EVEN ...SAVED... A SOUL ξ KLIK ξ

I WISH I COULD BELIEVE THAT, SMITH... I REALLY DO. BUT... I ... JUST CAN'T.

MAYBE THERE'S SOMETHING TO WHAT YOU SAID. BUT I'VE SEEN TOO MANY DEATHS IN MY TIME... TOO MANY LIVES WASTED NEEDLESSLY.

I'LL NEVER STOP BELIEVING THAT LIFE IS SOMETHING MOST SACRED, SOMETHING TO BE SACRIFICED ONLY FOR THAT GREATEST OF CAUSES ... LIBERTY!

NEXT ISSUE:

CAPTAIN AMERICA FOR PRESIDENT!

MARVEL COMICS GROUP

50¢ 250 OCT 02453

CAPTAIN AMERICA

HE'S THE PEOPLE'S CHOICE

CAPTAIN AMERICA FOR PRESIDENT!

HE IS ACROSS THE ROOM, VAULTING OVER THE MAKESHIFT BARRICADE IN AN INSTANT!

TO THE TERRORISTS, IT SEEMS ALMOST AS IF TIME IS STANDING STILL, THE AVENGER MOVES SO FAST!

AS THE FIRST GUNMAN GOES DOWN, HIS HOSTAGE MOUTHS A SILENT PRAYER AND DROPS TO THE FLOOR!

SEEMINGLY WITHOUT EFFORT, THIS ONE-MAN STRIKE FORCE TAKES OUT THE SECOND TERRORIST AND SETS HIS EYES ON THE THIRD.

AND THAT FINAL GUNMAN -- DESPITE HIS BOAST -- FEELS HIS BLOOD RUN COLD!

IN SUCH A SITUATION, MOST MEN WOULD HESITATE, FEARING TO MAKE ANOTHER MOVE, LEST THE HOSTAGE BE HARMED.

BUT THIS MAN IS THE VETERAN OF A THOUSAND BATTLES. HE KNOWS EXACTLY WHEN TO ACT, SO THAT THE LIFE IS SAVED...

BOAM

...AND THE TERROR IS ENDED!

HE IS CAPTAIN AMERICA! NO MORE NEED BE SAID!

THE BATTLE IS OVER... THREE-POINT SEVEN SECONDS AFTER IT BEGAN!

CONGRESSMAN GUNDERSEN? I'M AGENT ZIMMER... F.B.I. ARE YOU ALL RIGHT?

Y-YES, I BELIEVE SO. BUT IF CAPTAIN AMERICA HADN'T ARRIVED WHEN HE DID--!

I WAS GLAD TO LEND A HAND, SIR! IT'S JUST LUCKY I WAS IN THE AREA WHEN THIS RUCKUS STARTED!

THERE, THERE, MISS! IT'S ALL RIGHT!

N.P.

NPP

[62]

--AND TO FINALLY MEET YOU IN THE FLESH, AFTER ALL OF THESE YEARS... BOY, IT JUST DOES MY HEART PROUD!

WELL, MR. UNDERWOOD...

SAM! CALL ME SAM... EVERYBODY DOES! WELL, HERE WE ARE!

UNDERWOOD PUSHES OPEN A DOOR, AND...

BOYS, I WANT YOU TO MEET THE FELLA WHO PROBABLY SAVED OUR HIDES FROM A BUNCH OF TERRORISTS... *CAPTAIN AMERICA!*

COME ON, SAM... WHO'RE YOU KIDDIN'?

CHARLIE... HE'S NOT KIDDIN'!

IT'S HIM! IT'S REALLY HIM... CAPTAIN AMERICA!

IT SURE IS! CAP, I WANNA THANK YOU! YOU SAVED MY PLATOON A LOT OF GRIEF AT ANZIO!

I WAS IN THE BIG ONE, TOO, CAP... WITH PATTON'S BOYS! HEY, WERE YOU REALLY FROZEN IN ICE ALL THOSE YEARS?

YES, I...

YOU STILL LOOK LIKE A MILLION BUCKS, CAP! HEH... YOU EVER THINK OF RUNNING FOR OFFICE?

NOW, CHARLIE! I'M SURE CAP HAS ENOUGH ...TO... HMMM!

WAIT-A-MINUTE! SURE, THAT WOULD WORK! IT'D WORK LIKE A CHARM -- A FIFTY MILLION VOTE CHARM!

CAP, HOW WOULD YOU LIKE TO BE THE NEW POPULIST PARTY CANDIDATE FOR PRESIDENT?

HA-HAH! THANKS FOR THE OFFER, SAM-- BUT I'M AFRAID I'M NOT MUCH OF A POLITICIAN!

THE PEOPLE DON'T WANT A POLITICIAN... THEY WANT A LEADER!

SAM... YOU'RE SERIOUS, AREN'T YOU?

MINUTES LATER, IN THE BROOKLYN HEIGHTS APARTMENT OF STEVE ROGERS...

I STILL CAN'T BELIEVE THAT THEY'D CONSIDER RUNNING A CANDIDATE WHO HAS NO EXPERIENCE IN GOVERNMENT!

HMM... JUDGING FROM THE SHIFTING OF THE FLOOR-BOARDS, I'M ABOUT TO GET A VISITOR. I'D BETTER STASH MY SHIELD!

THAT'S THE NICE THING ABOUT OLDER BUILDINGS... THEY ALWAYS LET YOU KNOW WHEN COMPANY'S COMING!

GOOD MORNING, JOSH!

OH! 'MORNING STEVE! YOU READY FOR A DAY OF MANUAL LABOR?

I'VE BEEN LOOKING FORWARD TO IT!

GOOD! UH, SAY... BEFORE I FORGET AGAIN... THIS LETTER CAME FOR YOU THE OTHER DAY. LOOKS LIKE IT COULD BE IMPORTANT!

OH?

THIS IS SOME SORT OF QUESTION-NAIRE FROM THE DEPARTMENT OF THE ARMY, "WE ARE UPDATING OUR FILES ... PLEASE FILL OUT IN TRIPLICATE... ETCETERA, ETCETERA."

YEP, SAME OLD ARMY! SOME THINGS NEVER CHANGE!

--BUT KNOWING THE ARMY I DOUBT THAT IT'S VERY URGENT

I'LL FILL THIS OUT LATER, JOSH. I DON'T KNOW WHY THEY WANT ALL THIS INFO --

AND SO...

HAVE NO FEAR, LADY ROSENTHAL -- 'CAUSE COOPER AND ROGERS ARE HERE ON THE BALL! WE'LL MOVE YOU IN QUICK AND FAST AND ON TIME ... AND IT WON'T EVEN COST YOU ONE THIN DIME!

SO SPEAKS A GRADUATE OF THE MUHAMMAD ALI SCHOOL OF POETRY! HI, STEVE!

HELLO, BERNIE! I JUST HOPE OUR BUDDY'S BACK IS IN BETTER SHAPE THAN HIS VERSE ... LOOKS LIKE YOU HAVE QUITE A LOAD HERE!

INDEED, SEVERAL HOURS LATER...

MAN, I THOUGHT WE'D NEVER GET FINISHED! HOW DOES STEVE DO IT? HE'S CARRIED IN AT LEAST TWICE WHAT I DID, AND HE'S NOT EVEN BREATHING HEAVY!

THIS IS THE LAST OF THE BOXES, BERNIE, WHERE DO YOU WANT IT?

JUST SET IT DOWN ANYWHERE, STEVE. I'LL UNPACK EVERYTHING LATER.

IS THERE ANYTHING ELSE I CAN DO?

MMM...I CAN THINK OF SEVERAL THINGS! BUT FOR NOW, WHY DON'T YOU SIT DOWN AND HAVE SOME COFFEE?

THE COFFEE INSPIRES CONVERSATION, AND THE CONVERSATION TURNS TOWARD THE INEVITABLE TOPICS...

YEAH, I ALWAYS THOUGHT LOCAL ELECTIONS WERE MORE INTERESTING THAN NATIONAL. WHO DO YOU LIKE FOR CONGRESS, STEVE?

I'M EMBARRASSED TO ADMIT IT, BUT I'M NOT SURE WHO MY CONGRESSMAN IS!

ME, TOO -- AND I USED TO BE SO POLITICAL IN COLLEGE!

I'LL SAY! YOU WERE THE ORIGINAL CAMPUS ACTIVIST!

BUT WHAT DO YOU SAY WE CONTINUE THIS DEBATE OVER CHINESE FOOD?

HEY, IS THAT THE FAMOUS MIKE FARREL? NICE TO SEE YOU, MAN... NOW THAT EVERYTHING'S BEEN MOVED IN!

SORRY ABOUT THAT, COOP--

-- BUT I WAS INVOLVED IN ANOTHER POLITICAL DISCUSSION DOWN AT THE FIREHOUSE AND LOST ALL TRACK OF TIME!

YOU...TALKING POLITICS?! I DON'T BELIEVE IT! YOU'RE THE MOST APOLITICAL MAN I KNOW!

NORMALLY, MAYBE! BUT WHEN I HEARD THE NEWS--!

NEWS? WHAT NEWS?

OH, *NO!* I NEVER DREAMED THAT THIS NEW-POP PARTY WOULD DO THIS!

EVIDENTLY, THIS NEW-POP PARTY HAS CAP HALF-CONVINCED TO BE A CANDIDATE! IF THAT HAPPENS, I JUST MIGHT VOTE THIS YEAR!

YOU'RE TELLING ME THAT YOU *USUALLY* DON'T VOTE?

'FRAID SO, COOP! HECK, THERE'S NEVER ANYONE WORTH VOTING FOR! BUT IF CAP RUNS--!

I SEE WHAT YOU'RE SAYING! I KNOW I'D VOTE FOR THE MAN!

YOU WOULD, JOSH? YOU'D ACTUALLY VOTE FOR A MAN WHO IS BASICALLY ANONYMOUS... WHO WEARS A MASK?

HEY, BETTER THAN VOTING FOR SOME CROOK WHO DOESN'T WEAR A MASK!

WELL... UH... SURE, CAP HAS A REPUTATION FOR HONESTY-- BUT WHAT DOES HE KNOW ABOUT FOREIGN AFFAIRS, OR ENERGY, OR INFLATION--?

OH, STEVE! WHAT DO ANY OF THE CANDIDATES *REALLY* KNOW ABOUT THOSE THINGS?

WOULDN'T IT JUST BE GREAT TO HAVE A PRESIDENT YOU KNEW YOU COULD TRUST?

AND STEVE ROGERS FINDS HIMSELF NODDING RELUCTANTLY.

THE NEXT MORNING FINDS AN UNUSUAL AMOUNT OF ACTIVITY TAKING PLACE IN FRONT OF THE AVENGERS' FIFTH AVENUE MANSION.

THERE, A CROWD OF REPORTERS, CAMERAMEN, AND PASSERSBY AWAIT THE ARRIVAL OF ONE MAN...

HERE HE COMES! BRING UP THOSE CAMERAS... FAST!

HARV, SIGNAL THE STATION! I WANT TO GO LIVE WITH THIS!

CAP, WHEN WILL YOU BE ANNOUNCING YOUR INTENTIONS?

WHAT ARE YOUR VIEWS ON THE MID-EAST?

DO YOU THINK SOVIET EXPANSIONISM IS JUST A SCARE ISSUE?

WHAT ABOUT OPEC?

I'M HERE AT AVENGERS' MANSION, WHERE CAPTAIN AMERICA HAS JUST ARRIVED AMID GREAT PANDEMONIUM.

GENTLEMEN... LADIES... PLEASE!

[69]

I... UH... I'M IN A BIT OF A HURRY! AND I REALLY DON'T HAVE ANY-THING TO TELL YOU!

CAP!

CAP!

CAP, WHEN WILL YOU--?

LATER. ...ALL RIGHT?

MAYBE I *SHOULD* CALL A PRESS CONFERENCE... BEFORE THIS GETS TOTALLY OUT OF HAND!

HELLO, JARVIS! ANY WORLD-SHAKING MENACES ON SCHEDULE FOR TODAY?

NO, MASTER CAP, BUT THERE ARE A NUMBER OF TELEGRAMS FOR YOU!

WHAT'S THIS? THE REPUBLICANS WANT ME TO BE *THEIR* CANDIDATE? AND... AND THE DEMO-CRATS, TOO?!? THIS IS UNBELIEVABLE!

JARVIS, HAS THE WHOLE WORLD GONE CRAZY? WHAT NEXT?!

♪ HAPPY DAYS ARE HERE AGAIN! ♪♪

HIYA, CAPPY!

I HEARD THE GOOD NEWS, AND I'M READY TO HIT THE CAMPAIGN TRAIL! I CAN GUARANTEE THAT YOU'LL SWEEP THE *MUTANT* VOTE!

OH, NO!

AND THEN, OF COURSE THERE ARE MY LADY FRIENDS! THEIR VOTES ALONE SHOULD CARRY NEW YORK!

BEAST, I'M *NOT* A CANDIDATE!

NOT YET, MAYBE-- BUT YOU WILL BE! UH... WON'T YOU?

WHY ASK ME? I'M ONLY THE MAN WHO'S SUPPOSED TO BE RUNNING! WHO'D HAVE THOUGHT SO MANY PEOPLE WOULD BELIEVE WHAT THEY READ IN THE *GLOBE*?

IF ANYONE NEEDS ME, I'LL BE--

[70]

"--IN THE LIBRARY!"

WELL! IRON MAN... WASP... VISION... GOOD MORNING, ALL! WHAT BRINGS YOU HERE THIS MORNING?

ACTUALLY, WE WERE DISCUSSING YOU, CAP!

ARGUING IS MORE LIKE IT, IRON MAN! YOU'RE JUST IN TIME, CAP -- THEY WERE GANGING UP ON ME!

NOW, JAN... WE WERE MERELY POINTING OUT THE WEAKNESSES OF YOUR POSITION!

I'M SURE YOU CAN GUESS WHAT THIS COFFEE-KLATCH IS ALL ABOUT!

YOU'RE NOT SERIOUS ABOUT THIS PRESIDENTIAL NONSENSE, ARE YOU?

WELL, I'D HARDLY CALL THE PRESIDENCY "NONSENSE!" BUT--!

YOU TELL HIM, CAP! HE'S PROBABLY JEALOUS BECAUSE THEY DIDN'T ASK HIM!

THAT IS HARDLY A RATIONAL CONCLUSION, WASP! AFTER ALL, IRON MAN HAS ASKED TO STEP DOWN AS AVENGERS' CHAIRMAN... I HARDLY THINK HE HAS PUBLIC OFFICE IN MIND!

OH, I WAS JUST TEASING, VISION!

COME ON, CAP! YOU OF ALL PEOPLE SHOULD KNOW BETTER THAN TO GET MIXED UP IN POLITICS! YOU KNOW THE KIND OF RED TAPE AND CORRUPTION YOU'D BE FACED WITH!

YES, I KNOW--!

OH, DON'T LISTEN TO HIM! YOU'RE JUST THE KIND OF MAN THIS COUNTRY NEEDS! PEOPLE LOOK UP TO YOU... TRUST YOU! WHEN WAS THE LAST TIME WE HAD A PRESIDENT LIKE THAT?

THANK YOU, JAN, BUT--!

THE QUESTION IS NOT ONE OF RESPECT, BUT OF QUALIFICATIONS! YOU ARE A MAN OUT OF TIME, CAP... 1940'S SOLUTIONS WILL NOT WORK FOR TODAY'S PROBLEMS!

LOOK--

--NONE OF THIS CANDIDACY WAS MY IDEA! I APPRECIATE YOUR ADVICE, BUT I'M LIKE IRON MAN... I CAN'T BELIEVE ANYONE IS TAKING THIS SERIOUSLY!

PARDON ME, MASTER CAP, BUT THE WHITE HOUSE IS ON THE PHONE! THEY WISH TO KNOW IF YOU'LL BE NEEDING SECRET SERVICE PROTECTION!

WHAT?! YOU MEAN THE PRESIDENT CONSIDERS CAP A VIABLE CANDIDATE?

HE SHOULD, MASTER IRON MAN... HIS PARTY DOES!

WHAT SHOULD I TELL THEM, SIR?

TELL THEM... I HAVE A LOT OF THINKING TO DO, JARVIS!

MEANWHILE, ON THE SIDE-WALKS OF NEW YORK...

WE ASKED PASSERSBY THEIR REACTION TO REPORTS OF CAPTAIN AMERICA'S POSSIBLE CANDIDACY...

IT'S THE BEST NEWS I'VE HEARD SINCE THE MOON LANDING! I REMEMBER CAP FROM THE WAR YEARS! HE'S JUST WHAT WE NEED!

I'M SURE HE'D BE A GOOD LEADER, BUT WE KNOW SO LITTLE ABOUT HIM. WHERE DOES HE STAND ON MINORITY RIGHTS, ON AID TO EDUCA-TION, ON HOUSING?

GIMME A BREAK! THIS IS JUST ANOTHER ATTEMPT BY THE C.I.A. TO DEFRAUD THE ELECTORATE! I DON'T EVEN BELIEVE THERE IS A CAPTAIN AMERICA... I MEAN, I NEVER SEEN HIM!

BY THE NEXT DAY, THE SUBJECT OF CAP'S CANDIDACY IS ON THE MINDS OF ALL MANNER OF PEOPLE...

WHAT DO YA THINK, NICK?

DUM-DUM, I THINK I'D BETTER MAKE SURE I'M REGISTERED!

WELL, HE'D PROBABLY MAKE A BETTER PRESI-DENT THAN FOGGY MADE A DISTRICT ATTORNEY!

FUNNY, I NEVER THOUGHT OF CAP AS THE POLITICAL TYPE!

INTERESTING, I PRAY TO THE VISHANTI THAT HE MAKES THE RIGHT DECISION.

AND, IN THE OFFICES OF NEW YORK'S DAILY BUGLE...

WHAT'S THE WORD, JONAH? WILL WE ENDORSE CAP IF HE DECIDES TO RUN?

J. JONAH JAMESON FOUNDER & PUBLISHER

WAR!

KENNEDY SHOT IN DALLAS

I DON'T KNOW, ROBBIE... I JUST DON'T KNOW.

CAP'S A GOOD MAN... BUT YOU REMEMBER WHAT HAPPENED WHEN MOVIE STARS STARTED RUNNING FOR OFFICE!

IT WAS LIKE OPENING A FLOOD GATE! IT SEEMED LIKE THEY WERE ALL RUNNING FOR SOMETHING!

IF CAP SHOULD RUN, LORD KNOWS WHO ELSE WOULD! I CAN SEE IT NOW... IRON MAN FOR GOVERNOR... MR. FANTASTIC FOR SENATOR!

OR EVEN SPIDER-MAN FOR MAYOR, EH?

WHAT ?!?

I TAKE IT, THEN, THAT WE WON'T BE ENDORSING HIM!

AND, AS TWILIGHT OVERTAKES THE CITY, THE MAN-OF-THE-HOUR FINDS HIMSELF TRAVERSING THE ROOFTOPS OF THE LOWER EAST SIDE... IN SEARCH OF AN ANSWER.

I HAD NO IDEA THE PUBLIC REACTION WOULD BE LIKE THIS!

I'M FLATTERED THAT SO MANY PEOPLE THINK I'D MAKE A GOOD PRESIDENT... BUT HOW COULD I POSSIBLY RUN?

I'VE FINALLY GOTTEN MY PRIVATE LIFE SAILING ON AN EVEN KEEL. IF I WERE PRESIDENT, IT WOULD BE LIKE ASSUMING A NEW IDENTITY...

...THERE'D BE NO TIME FOR STEVE ROGERS OR CAPTAIN AMERICA-- JUST "MR. PRESIDENT!"

HEY, THAT OLD ABANDONED BUILDING... I KNOW THAT PLACE!

THAT'S THE BUILDING WHERE STEVE ROGERS ATTENDED SCHOOL, BACK IN THE THIRTIES! FROM THE LOOKS OF IT, IT'S BEEN CONDEMNED FOR SOME TIME!

IT'S A WONDER THAT IT'S STILL STANDING. THE CITY MUST NOT HAVE BEEN ABLE TO AFFORD TO TEAR IT DOWN!

BOY, DOES THIS BRING BACK THE MEMORIES!

FOR SEVERAL MINUTES, THE AVENGER STANDS STOCK STILL, AWASH IN HIS OWN THOUGHTS, AND THEN...

I JUST HAVE TO TAKE A LOOK AROUND. THIS PLACE WAS A PART OF ME FOR SO MANY YEARS!

[73]

WELL, I'LL BE--! SOME OF THE DESKS ARE STILL IN PLACE! IT SEEMS LIKE ONLY YESTERDAY I WAS A STUDENT HERE!

I CAN STILL RECALL SITTING IN THAT FRONT-ROW SEAT, AS MRS. CROSLEY TRIED TO SHOVE SOME KNOWLEDGE INTO OUR HEADS! SHE WAS A TOUGH TEACHER... BUT FAIR. I CAN ALMOST SEE HER--

"-- STANDING THERE RAMROD STRAIGHT AT THE BLACKBOARD!"

IF YOU GIRLS WILL STOP PASSING NOTES FOR A MINUTE, I'D LIKE TO REMIND YOU ABOUT THE CIVICS TEST NEXT WEEK!

CIVICS TEST MONDAY

I HOPE THAT YOUR SCORES WILL BE HIGHER THIS TIME!

YOU KNOW, YOU CHILDREN ARE VERY LUCKY TO BE LIVING IN A COUNTRY AS FREE AS THIS ONE! THE UNITED STATES OFFERS ITS CITIZENS MORE RIGHTS THAN ANY OTHER NATION IN THE WORLD!

BUT ALONG WITH THOSE RIGHTS COME CERTAIN DUTIES AS WELL!

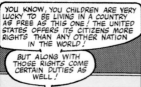

IT'S THE DUTY OF EACH ONE OF YOU TO SEE THAT THIS LAND STAYS FREE... TO SEE THAT JUSTICE IS EXTENDED TO ALL!

NOW, I KNOW THAT MANY OF YOUR FAMILY ARE HAVING A HARD TIME MAKING ENDS MEET...

...AND THINGS MAY WELL GET WORSE BEFORE THEY GET BETTER... BUT I HAVE FAITH THAT THEY WILL GET BETTER!

JUST AS I HAVE FAITH THAT YOU WILL COME TO THE AID OF YOUR COUNTRY WHEN DUTY CALLS. I PRAY THAT YOU DO THE RIGHT THING... THE BRAVE THING.

PLEASE DON'T LET ME DOWN.

I... I WON'T, MRS. CROSLEY.

[74]

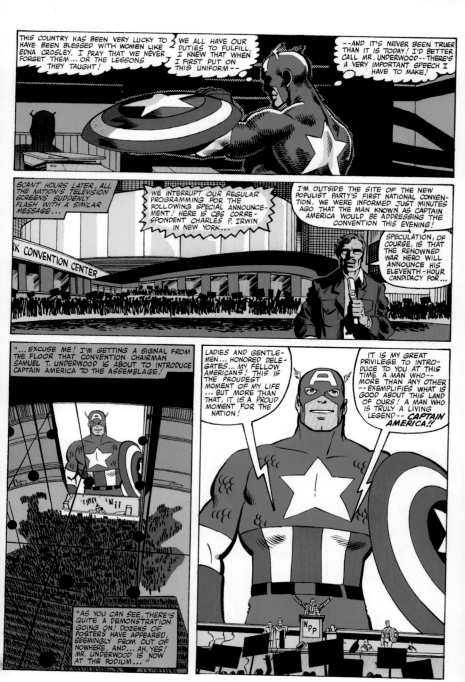

THIS COUNTRY HAS BEEN VERY LUCKY TO HAVE BEEN BLESSED WITH WOMEN LIKE EDNA CROSLEY. I PRAY THAT WE NEVER FORGET THEM... OR THE LESSONS THEY TAUGHT!

WE ALL HAVE OUR DUTIES TO FULFILL. I KNEW THAT WHEN I FIRST PUT ON THIS UNIFORM--

--AND IT'S NEVER BEEN TRUER THAN IT IS TODAY! I'D BETTER CALL MR. UNDERWOOD--THERE'S A VERY IMPORTANT SPEECH I HAVE TO MAKE!

SCANT HOURS LATER, ALL THE NATION'S TELEVISION SCREENS SUDDENLY FLASH WITH A SIMILAR MESSAGE...

WE INTERRUPT OUR REGULAR PROGRAMMING FOR THE FOLLOWING SPECIAL ANNOUNCE-MENT! HERE IS CBS CORRE-SPONDENT CHARLES P. IRWIN IN NEW YORK...

I'M OUTSIDE THE SITE OF THE NEW POPULIST PARTY'S FIRST NATIONAL CONVEN-TION. WE WERE INFORMED JUST MINUTES AGO THAT THE MAN KNOWN AS CAPTAIN AMERICA WOULD BE ADDRESSING THE CONVENTION THIS EVENING!

SPECULATION, OF COURSE, IS THAT THE RENOWNED WAR HERO WILL ANNOUNCE HIS ELEVENTH-HOUR CANDIDACY FOR...

RK CONVENTION CENTER

"...EXCUSE ME! I'M GETTING A SIGNAL FROM THE FLOOR THAT CONVENTION CHAIRMAN SAMUEL T. UNDERWOOD IS ABOUT TO INTRODUCE CAPTAIN AMERICA TO THE ASSEMBLAGE!"

LADIES AND GENTLE-MEN... HONORED DELE-GATES... MY FELLOW AMERICANS! THIS IS THE PROUDEST MOMENT OF MY LIFE ...BUT MORE THAN THAT, IT IS A PROUD MOMENT FOR THE NATION!

IT IS MY GREAT PRIVILEGE TO INTRO-DUCE TO YOU AT THIS TIME A MAN WHO-- MORE THAN ANY OTHER --EXEMPLIFIES WHAT IS GOOD ABOUT THIS LAND OF OURS! A MAN WHO IS TRULY A LIVING LEGEND-- *CAPTAIN AMERICA!!*

"AS YOU CAN SEE, THERE'S QUITE A DEMONSTRATION GOING ON! DOZENS OF POSTERS HAVE APPEARED, SEEMINGLY FROM OUT OF NOWHERE, AND... AH, YES! MR. UNDERWOOD IS NOW AT THE PODIUM..."

N Pp

[75]

THE ARENA ERUPTS INTO A GREAT CACOPHONY OF CHEERS AND APPLAUSE. IT IS SEVERAL MINUTES BEFORE THE RED-WHITE-AND-BLUE AVENGER CAN MAKE HIMSELF BE HEARD!

FRIENDS! PLEASE, MAY I HAVE YOUR ATTENTION! WHAT I HAVE TO SAY WILL NOT TAKE LONG... BUT I HOPE IT WILL BE MEANINGFUL!

AS YOU'RE ALL WELL AWARE, THERE HAS BEEN A LOT OF TALK THESE PAST FEW DAYS... TALK TRIGGERED BY CERTAIN STORIES APPEARING IN THE PRESS.

I HAVE GIVEN MUCH THOUGHT TO THOSE STORIES... AND TO THE PUBLIC DISCUSSION THEY INSPIRED. I HAVE HAD TO FACE THE QUESTION OF WHETHER OR NOT I SHOULD BE A CANDIDATE FOR PRESIDENT OF THE UNITED STATES.

YOU'RE THE MAN, CAP!

YAY YAY YAH YAY YAY

ONCE AGAIN, CAP MUST WAIT FOR THE TUMULT TO DIE DOWN...

AS I WAS SAYING, I GAVE THIS MUCH THOUGHT ... AND I HAVE COME TO MY DECISION.

THE PRESIDENCY IS ONE OF THE MOST IMPORTANT JOBS IN THE WORLD. THE HOLDER OF THAT OFFICE MUST REPRESENT THE BEST INTERESTS OF AN ENTIRE NATION.

NPP

HE MUST BE READY TO NEGOTIATE -- TO COMPROMISE -- 24 HOURS A DAY, TO PRESERVE THE REPUBLIC AT ALL COSTS!

-- I HAVE WORKED AND FOUGHT ALL MY LIFE FOR THE GROWTH AND ADVANCEMENT OF THE AMERICAN DREAM. AND I BELIEVE THAT MY DUTY TO THE *DREAM* WOULD SEVERELY LIMIT ANY ABILITIES I MIGHT HAVE TO PRESERVE THE REALITY.

I UNDERSTAND THIS... I APPRECIATE THIS... AND I REALIZE THE NEED TO WORK WITHIN SUCH A FRAMEWORK. BY THE SAME TOKEN--

WE MUST ALL LIVE IN THE REAL WORLD... AND SOMETIMES THAT WORLD CAN BE PRETTY GRIM. BUT IT IS THE DREAM... THE HOPE... THAT MAKES THE REALITY WORTH LIVING.

IN THE EARLY 1940'S, I MADE A PERSONAL PLEDGE TO UPHOLD THE DREAM... AND AS LONG AS THE DREAM REMAINS EVEN PARTIALLY UNFULFILLED, I CANNOT ABANDON IT!

AND SO I HOPE YOU CAN UNDERSTAND--

50¢
251
NOV
02453
MARVEL® COMICS GROUP
COMICS CODE AUTHORITY
CAPTAIN AMERICA
©1980 MARVEL COMICS GROUP
THE MERCENARY AND THE MADMAN!

STAN LEE PRESENTS: CAPTAIN AMERICA!

THE MERCENARY AND THE MADMAN

SUNSET...A TIME FOR SOLEMN REFLECTION!

IF YOUR NAME IS CAPTAIN AMERICA, THOSE REFLECTIONS COVER COUNTLESS MILES...AND SEVERAL DECADES!

INCREDIBLE! SOMETIMES I CAN HARDLY BELIEVE HOW NEW YORK HAS CHANGED SINCE I GREW UP HERE IN THE 1930'S!

SO MUCH OF MY LIFE SEEMS LIKE SOME SORT OF AMAZING DREAM...

...BUT IN MY HEART I KNOW THAT THE GREATEST DREAM STILL LIES AHEAD!

BEGINNING: AN ALL-NEW EXCURSION INTO THE LIFE AND TIMES OF AMERICA'S LIVING LEGEND, AS CHRONICLED BY:

ROGER STERN
WRITER

JOHN BYRNE
PENCILER

JOSEF RUBINSTEIN
INKER

JIM NOVAK
LETTERER

BOB SHAREN
COLORIST

JIM SALICRUP
EDITOR

JIM SHOOTER
FLAG-WAVER

THE DREAM BEGINS... NOW!

EVER SINCE I -- HOW WOULD THE *BEAST* PUT IT?-- GOT MY HEAD TOGETHER,* MY MEMORIES OF GROWING UP DURING THE GREAT DEPRESSION HAVE ALL COME BACK TO ME SO VIVIDLY!

I WAS THE ORIGINAL 98-POUND WEAKLING IN THOSE DAYS... BEFORE I VOLUNTEERED TO BE THE GUINEA PIG FOR OPERATION REBIRTH, AND DR. ERSKINE'S SERUM TRANSFORMED ME INTO AMERICA'S SUPER-SOLDIER!

I WAS PROUD TO SERVE MY COUNTRY AS CAPTAIN AMERICA. THE PRESERVATION OF FREEDOM WAS AN IMPORTANT DUTY DURING THOSE DARK DAYS OF WORLD WAR TWO.

WHO COULD HAVE GUESSED BACK THEN, THAT A FREAK ACCIDENT WOULD THROW ME INTO SUSPENDED ANIMATION AT WAR'S END,... THAT I'D SPEND SEVERAL DECADES FROZEN IN A BLOCK OF ICE... LOST TO MOST OF THE WORLD!

*SEE ISSUE #247 -- JIM.

"I MIGHT STILL BE UP THERE IN THE ARCTIC -- A FROZEN FIGURE, WORSHIPPED BY ESKIMOS, IF IT HADN'T BEEN FOR ONE MAN... "

HEAR ME, HUMANS! THIS IS NO HELPLESS TOTEM YOU SEE BEFORE YOU! THIS IS THE *SUB-MARINER*, WHO HAS SWORN VENGEANCE UPON THE ENTIRE HUMAN RACE!

IT IS THE DREADED *NAMOR* -- THE LEGENDARY ONE!

RUN, YOU WEAK, HELPLESS MORTALS! FLEE IN TERROR BEFORE THE RIGHTFUL WRATH OF NAMOR! THUS SHALL *ALL* OF MANKIND ONE DAY SHRIEK IN PANIC AT THE COMING OF THE SUB-MARINER!

*"IF A TERRIFIED ESKIMO HADN'T STUMBLED INTO A U.S. WEATHER STATION A FEW DAYS LATER AND BLURTED OUT THE STORY, I MIGHT NEVER HAVE FOUND OUT WHO WAS RESPONSIBLE FOR MY 'RESURRECTION'!"

TAKE YOUR ACCURSED IDOL *WITH* YOU! *GO --* SPREAD THE WORD -- LET THE WORLD KNOW THAT NAMOR IS *STILL* A FORCE TO BE RECKONED WITH!

"SOMEHOW, IT SEEMED ALMOST FITTING THAT NAMOR, WHO HAD BEEN MY ALLY DURING THE WAR, SHOULD BE THE ONE TO FREE ME... KNOWINGLY OR NOT!"

"I GUESS IT WAS JUST LUCK THAT I FLOATED INTO THE WARM WATERS OF THE GULF STREAM, WHERE MY ICY PRISON SLOWLY MELTED AWAY..."

"... AND I DRIFTED PAST AN UNDER-SEA CRAFT MANNED BY THE *AVENGERS!*"

I'VE GOT HIM!

WHO CAN HE *BE*? WHY IS HE FROZEN SOLID?

LOOK, GIANT-MAN! BENEATH HIS TATTERED CLOTHES-- HE WEARS SOME SORT OF COLORFUL COSTUME!

CAN THIS REALLY BE THE FAMOUS SHIELD OF THE ONCE-MIGHTY CRIME FIGHTER?

WAIT! DON'T YOU *RECOGNIZE* IT?? IT'S THE FAMOUS RED, WHITE, AND BLUE GARB OF --*CAPTAIN AMERICA!*

THE WASP IS *RIGHT!*

LOOK AT THIS, THOR... HIS FACE MASK --WITH THE PROUD LETTER "A" ON IT! IT *MUST* BE HIM!

"IF THE AVENGERS WERE SURPRISED TO FIND ME, THEY WERE EVEN MORE SURPRISED TO DISCOVER THAT I WAS STILL ALIVE!"

"I OWE THEM A LOT. THEY LET ME JOIN THEM ... GAVE MY LIFE PURPOSE...

--WHILE I TRIED TO ADJUST TO THIS BRAVE NEW WORLD I FOUND MYSELF IN!"

"OF COURSE, I WASN'T THE ONLY ONE TO HAVE SURVIVED THE PASSING OF DECADES! MY OLDEST FOE, THE RED SKULL, HAD ALSO FALLEN INTO A STATE OF SUSPENDED ANIMATION!"

"WHEN HE FINALLY AWOKE, OUR PRIVATE WAR RESUMED... EVENTUALLY AFFECTING THE LIVES OF THE NEW ALLIES I HAD MADE --

"-- LIKE SAM WILSON, THE *FALCON!* SAM WAS A GOOD FRIEND AND PARTNER...

...BUT THE DAY CAME WHEN HE HAD TO GO OUT ON HIS OWN!"

AND THEN, THERE WAS SHARON CARTER... CERTAINLY THE LOVELIEST S.H.I.E.L.D.* AGENT I EVER WORKED ALONGSIDE. WE WERE CLOSE FOR SUCH A SHORT TIME IN THE BIG PICTURE... HER DEATH STILL HURTS!

SHE WAS THE ONE TRUE LOVE IN THIS SECOND LIFE OF MINE. I'LL NEVER FORGET HER!

*SUPREME HEADQUARTERS INTERNATIONAL ESPIONAGE LAW-ENFORCEMENT DIVISION -- JIM.

[81]

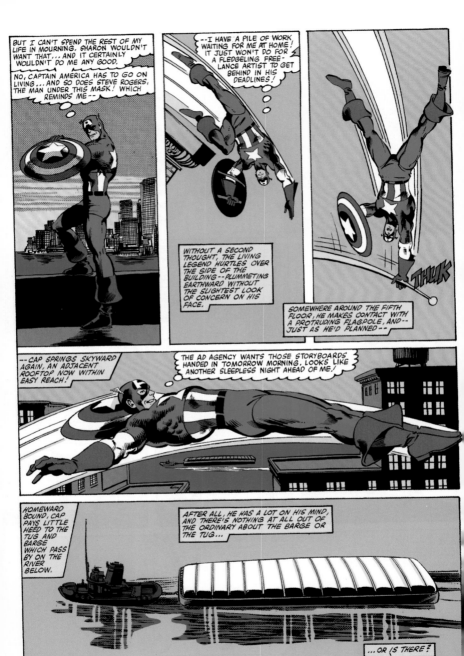

CERTAINLY, THE TUG'S CREW SEEMS COMMON ENOUGH... BUT THEIR DESTINATION IS SOMETHING QUITE UNUSUAL!

WE'RE CLOSING FAST ON RYKER'S ISLAND... PASS THE WORD!

GOTCHA!

RYKER'S ISLAND... AN ISOLATED ROCK IN THE MIDDLE OF LONG ISLAND SOUND... AND THE HOME OF A NEW YORK STATE PENITENTIARY!

LIKE THE BARGE, THE PRISON APPEARS ORDINARY ENOUGH. HOWEVER, SOME OF ITS INMATES ARE ANYTHING BUT ORDINARY!

AND AS THE TUG DRAWS NEARER TO THE ISLAND--

--THE ACTIVITY ON ITS DECK BECOMES QUITE EXTRAORDINARY!

IT'S TIME! UNWRAP THE SAPPER!

MAN, THIS GIZMO IS SOMETHIN' ELSE! WHAT KINDA MIND COMES UP WITH STUFF LIKE THIS?

THE KINDA MIND WE'RE BUSTIN' OUTTA HERE! THE JOE WHO DESIGNED THIS SUCKER IS STUCK ON THE INSIDE--

--SO IT'S ONLY FAIR THAT WE USE HIS GEAR TO GET HIM OUT!

THE DISH-LIKE PROJECTOR ERUPTS WITH A BLINDING WHITE GLARE WHICH ALMOST INSTANTLY DISSOLVES INTO THE INFRA-RED END OF THE LIGHT SPECTRUM--

--BATHING THE ISLAND IN AN EERIE BEAM WHICH SAPS THE POWER AWAY FROM EVERY ELECTRICAL DEVICE IN ITS FIELD!

AND, AS THE ISLAND GOES DARK, THE SIDE OF THE BARGE SUDDENLY OPENS UP -- DIS-CHARGING A SMALL BAND OF COMMANDO RAIDERS!

COME ON, WE DON'T HAVE MUCH TIME! FAN OUT AND WATCH FOR GUARDS!

WITH A SPEED RIVALING THAT OF A CRACK SPECIAL FORCES UNIT, THE COMMANDOES POUR THROUGH THE PRISON PERIMETER --

BOAM

--THE NIGHT-VISION LENSES OF THEIR MASKS GLISTENING WEIRDLY IN THE DARKNESS!

WHAT LITTLE OPPOSITION THEY MEET IS INSTANTLY SILENCED BY A HAIL OF BULLETS --

P-P-PTOW

--OR A CANNISTER OF SLEEP-GAS!

WITHIN SECONDS, THEY ARE HALFWAY THROUGH THE MAIN BUILDING, HEADING TOWARDS THEIR OBJECTIVE LIKE AN UNSTOPPABLE JUGGERNAUT!

C'MON! IT'S JUST AHEAD!

THIS GUY WON'T GIVE US ANY MORE TROUBLE! THE CELL BLOCK IS OURS... GET THE GEAR READY!

KRAK

BLOCK EIGHT

[84]

CELL BLOCK EIGHT-- ONE OF THE MOST HEAVILY FORTIFIED MAXIMUM SECURITY PRISON AREAS ON THE EASTERN SEABOARD! HERE THE WALLS ARE THREE TIMES THE NORMAL THICKNESS, REINFORCED WITH SLABS OF OMNIUM STEEL... HERE EACH CELL IS ESPECIALLY DESIGNED TO HOLD ITS OCCUPANT!

WHAT'S GOING ON?

IT'S A BREAK! GET ME OUTTA HERE!

ME! TAKE ME!

SHUT UP! WE ONLY HAVE TIME TO SPRING ONE GUY...

... AND HERE HE IS!

SIR! GET ON YOUR BUNK AND COVER YOUR EARS!

TWO SECONDS TICK BY AS A SPECIAL BAZOOKA IS SET UP, AND THEN...

FIRE!

KRAKOW

THE ROCKET SHELL DOES NOT EVEN PIERCE THE MASSIVE CELL DOOR, BUT IT DOES ITS JOB!

SIR? ARE YOU ALL RIGHT?

ANOTHER IN-MATE WOULD HAVE BEEN KNOCKED COLD BY THE CONCUSSION SHOCK... BUT NOT THIS MAN!

THIS IS THE SUPER-CRIMINAL KNOWN AS MISTER HYDE!

G-GOOD! YOU... CAME ...AT LAST!

¿UNNGH! THE INFO THE BOSS GOT WAS ON THE LEVEL! THEY MUST'VE GIVEN HYDE ENOUGH DRUGS TO KNOCK OUT AN ELEPHANT!

FIGURES! HE WEIGHS ABOUT AS MUCH AS ONE!

NO TIME TO TALK! THERE'S ONLY ABOUT A MIN-UTE LEFT BEFORE THE SAPPER BURNS ITSELF OUT!

MINUTES LATER, THE POWER SUDDENLY RETURNS TO RYKER'S ISLAND.

AND AMID THE RESULTANT PANDEMONIUM IN THE PRISON, NO ONE NOTICES THE INNOCENT-LOOKING TUG AND BARGE WHICH SLOWLY PULL AWAY!

BUT, BENEATH THE DECEPTIVE FAÇADE OF THE BARGE...

WELL, MONSIEUR-- I TRUST YOU ARE FEELING BETTER NOW, NON?

Y-YES! THEY KEPT ME DOPED-UP FOR SO LONG... TO PREVENT MY ESCAPING... IT'S A RELIEF TO STAND ON MY OWN TWO FEET AGAIN!

THIS... IS QUITE AN ELABORATE LITTLE FLOATING HEADQUARTERS YOU HAVE HERE! BUT I WOULD EXPECT NO LESS OF--

--BATROC THE LEAPER!

MAIS CERTAINEMENT, MONSIEUR! AND MIGHT I RETURN THE COMPLIMENT? YOUR POWER-SAPPER MADE ENGINEERING YOUR ESCAPE CHILD'S PLAY! A PITY IT HAD TO BURN OUT... AS YOU WARNED US IT WOULD!

BAH! IT WAS JUST AN EXPERI-MENTAL MODEL! YOU FOUND MY HIDDEN CACHE OF EQUIPMENT WITHOUT ANY TROUBLE, THEN? EVERYTHING WAS IN ORDER?

WE FOUND IT ALL, EXACTLY AS YOU LEFT IT, M'SIEUR! THE INSTRUCTIONS YOU SENT OUT VIA THE PRISON GRAPEVINE, THOUGH IN CODE, WERE CLEARER THAN CLEAR TO THE GREAT BATROC!

AH! ALLOW ME TO INTRO-DUCE MY-- HOW YOU SAY --COMPANION... MADAMOI-SELLE MONIQUE!

'ALLO, MONSIEUR!

HER ENGLISH IS NOT SO GOOD, I AM AFRAID!

BATROC, YOU IMPRESS ME... AND HYDE IS IMPRESSED BY FEW MEN! YOUR CREW CARRIED OUT MY RESCUE WITH COMMENDABLE DISPATCH!

BUT OF COURSE, MON AMI! AFTER I LEARNED THROUGH VARIOUS SOURCES THAT YOU WISHED TO ESCAPE, I HAD NEARLY A WEEK TO PLAN THE BREAKOUT!

EXCUSE MOI, M'SIEUR HYDE... BUT YOU WILL BE MORE COMFORTABLE WEARING YOUR OWN ATTIRE, NON?

AH, THIS IS MUCH BETTER! I'D ALMOST FORGOTTEN WHAT IT WAS LIKE TO WEAR SOMETHING BESIDES PRISON GREYS!

I CAN WELL IMAGINE! NOW... ABOUT THAT FIVE MILLION DOLLARS YOU PROMISED TO WHOMEVER WOULD ENGINEER YOUR FREEDOM... IS IT CLOSE BY?

CLOSE BY? HAH-HAH! IT DOESN'T EVEN EXIST YET!

WHAT ?!

PIG! YOU DARE TO DECEIVE THE MIGHTY BAT--

--ROC?

KRUNCH

DO NOT USE THAT TONE OF VOICE WITH ME, BATROC! MISTER HYDE DARES MANY THINGS!

MINE IS THE POWER WHICH CAUSED EVEN THE MIGHTY THOR TO TREMBLE!

I DOUBT THAT, HYDE--

-- JUST AS I DOUBT THAT YOU CAN DEFEAT WHAT YOU CANNOT STRIKE!

AND BATROC HAS NOT SPENT HALF OF HIS CAREER BEHIND BARS, AS YOU HAVE! NOW... LET US SEE WHAT GOOD YOUR POWER IS AGAINST A MASTER OF THE ART OF *LA SAVATE!*

OH!

HAH! I'VE HEARD OF THIS STRANGE FOOT-FIGHTING! YOU PEOPLE ARE A FUNNY RACE!

NOM DÛN CHIEN! THAT BLOW WOULD HAVE LEFT A NORMAL MAN PARA-LYZED FOR DAYS!

I AM HARDLY A NORMAL MAN, BATROC!

MON DIEU! HIS SPEED IS NEARLY THE EQUAL OF MY OWN! I WOULD NOT HAVE BELIEVED A MAN OF SUCH SIZE COULD REACT SO FAST!

NOW LISTEN TO ME, YOU GALLIC FOOL! I COULD MAKE GOOD USE OF A SMALL GROUP OF WELL-TRAINED MEN.

IF YOU AND YOUR CREW THROW IN WITH ME, YOU'LL HAVE RICHES THAT'LL MAKE MY OFFER OF FIVE MILLION LOOK LIKE PEANUTS!

I-I HAD NOT PLANNED ON ANY EXTENDED PARTNERSHIPS...

[88]

...B-BUT YOUR ARGUMENT IS... MOST... CONVINCING!

IF YOU WOULD JUST LET ME DOWN, I WOULD BE MOST INTERESTED IN HEARING ANY PLANS YOU MIGHT HAVE!

I KNEW YOU'D SEE IT MY WAY! WAIT! IS THIS THE MOST RECENT COPY OF THE *DAILY BUGLE*?

M-MAIS OUI, IT IS TODAY'S EDITION!

IN THAT CASE, I THINK THIS HEADLINE STORY WILL PROVIDE US WITH ALL THE INFORMATION WE'LL NEED TO BECOME VERY WEALTHY MEN... AND IN LESS THAN TWENTY-FOUR HOURS!

PERHAPS... BUT I SHALL BE WATCHING YOU VERY CLOSELY FOR EACH ONE OF THOSE HOURS, M'SIEUR!

TIME PASSES, AND MORNING FINALLY COMES TO THE NEW YORK AREA!

AND, TO ONE RESIDENT OF THIS BROOKLYN HEIGHTS APARTMENT BUILDING, A FULL NIGHT OF WORK IS NEARLY OVER...

THERE! ONE MORE LINE AND...

...I'M DONE! NOT A BAD JOB, IF I DO SAY SO MYSELF!

KNOCK-KNOCK! ANYBODY HOME?

COME ON IN, BERNIE -- IT'S UNLOCKED!

SO I NOTICED! YOU'RE A TRUSTING SOUL, STEVE ROGERS!

NOW LET ME GUESS... FROM THE SLIGHT REDNESS IN YOUR EYES AND THE WISPY STUBBLE ON YOUR CHIN, I'D SAY YOU'VE BEEN UP ALL NIGHT!

AH, YOU'RE TOO CLEVER FOR ME, MS. ROSENTHAL... YOU'VE FOUND ME OUT AGAIN!

IN THAT CASE, I'M FIXING YOU BREAKFAST! WELL, DON'T JUST STAND THERE -- GO SHAVE OR SOMETHING! GO ON --MOVE IT!

YOU WOULDN'T BY ANY CHANCE BE RELATED TO A GENTLEMAN BY THE NAME OF DUFFY, WOULD YOU?

WHO?

PRIVATE JOKE! HE WAS MY OLD ARMY SERGEANT!

I NEVER KNEW YOU WERE IN THE ARMY! WERE YOU IN 'NAM?

UH... I WAS THERE BRIEFLY!

NOT BRIEFLY ENOUGH, I'LL BET! MY COUSIN WAS IN THE MEKONG DELTA FOR SIX MONTHS!

STEVEN ROGERS!! PRACTICALLY EVERYTHING IN YOUR CUPBOARD IS "INSTANT SOMETHING!" DON'T YOU EVER EAT REAL FOOD?

WHENEVER I CAN! THE PROBLEM IS THAT... WELL, I'M ON THE GO A LOT, AND I DON'T WANT TO KEEP STUFF AROUND THAT'LL SPOIL!

DO YOU MIND IF I PUT ON SOME MUSIC?

NO, GO AHEAD!

WHAT'S THIS? ARTIE SHAW... TOMMY DORSEY... SINATRA... GLENN MILLER?!

STEVE, YOU HAVE THE STRANGEST TASTE IN MUSIC! IT'S JUST LIKE MY FATHER'S!

REALLY? WELL, I KNOW I DON'T HAVE MUCH IN THE WAY OF RECORDS... I JUST KEEP THE STUFF I LIKE, I THINK THERE ARE SOME BROADWAY SHOW TUNES IN THERE SOMEWHERE!

NEVER MIND. I'LL JUST SWITCH ON THE RADIO. THERE'LL BE SOMETHING GOOD ON THE...

...F-M.

STEVE? WHO'S THE PRETTY BLONDE? YOUR SISTER?

I HOPE.

WHO? OH... SHARON. NO, SHARON WAS... A VERY CLOSE, VERY DEAR... FRIEND.

WE TALKED ABOUT GETTING MARRIED ONCE, BUT OUR CAREERS ALWAYS SEEMED TO GET IN THE WAY!

SHE... DIED RECENTLY. IT HAPPENED QUITE SUDDENLY.

BOY, DID I EVER SAY THE WRONG THING! SHE MUST HAVE MEANT A LOT TO HIM.

THE AIR'S SO THICK IN HERE, YOU CAN CUT IT! I'D BETTER CHANGE THE SUBJECT, QUICK!

UH, DID YOU HEAR ABOUT THE BIG BREAKOUT AT RYKER'S ISLAND?

YOU MEAN, THE COBRA'S BIG ESCAPE? *

NO, THAT WAS LAST WEEK! I'M TALKING ABOUT LAST NIGHT! OH, LISTEN... MAYBE THE NEWS WILL HAVE SOMETHING ABOUT IT!

*SEE SPECTACULAR SPIDER-MAN #46. --J.S.

AUTHORITIES ARE STILL BAFFLED AS TO EXACTLY HOW POWER WAS CUT OFF TO RYKER'S ISLAND BY THE SMALL BAND WHICH BROKE IN AND MADE OFF WITH THE NOTORIOUS MR. HYDE!

WHAT?! FIRST THE COBRA BREAKS FREE, AND NOW HYDE, TOO? I'D BETTER--!

NO, WHAT AM I THINKING OF? I CAN'T GO CHASING AFTER EVERY-ONE WHO BREAKS OUT OF PRISON ... ESPECIALLY NOW! I HAVEN'T SLEPT IN OVER THIRTY HOURS--

--AND I HAVE TO GET THAT AD JOB TURNED IN TODAY!

BOTH THOR AND DAREDEVIL HAVE HAD MORE EXPERIENCE FIGHTING HYDE. IF THEY CAN'T FIND HIM, THEN I'LL OFFER MY HELP TO THE POLICE!

BREAKFAST IS SERVED!

LOOKS GREAT! I HOPE YOU'LL BE JOINING ME!

I WOULDN'T MISS IT FOR THE WORLD!

YOU KNOW, I HATE TO BRAG, BUT I MAKE A PRETTY MEAN BREAKFAST. OF COURSE, IT'S HARD TO RUIN EGGS!

OH, I'VE SEEN IT DONE! NO, BERNA-DETTE, I'D SAY YOU'RE A VERY ACCOMPLISHED COOK! TELL ME, DO YOU DO THIS FOR A LIVING?

NO, KIND SIR... I'M A GLASS-BLOWER!

OH... REALLY?

YES... REALLY!

ONE HEARTY BREAKFAST, A LITTLE SMALL TALK, AND THIRTY MINUTES LATER, STEVE ROGERS IS ON THE SUBWAY, MANHATTAN BOUND...

WITNESSES TO THE PRISON BREAK-IN SAY TWO OF THE RAIDERS HAD SLIGHT FRENCH ACCENTS! THE D.A.'S OFFICE HAS ENTERED THE INVESTIGATION...

FRENCH?

AND SOON, AT THE PLUMMER AD AGENCY...

I TELL YA, STEVIE, THESE STORYBOARDS ARE JUST THE WAY I WANTED 'EM! I DON'T KNOW WHO WAS LUCKIER THE DAY YOU TALKED THAT WINDBAG PLUMMER INTO GIVIN' YOU WORK ...YOU OR ME!

STEVE? HEY, ROGERS!

HUH? OH, SORRY, CARMINE... I GUESS MY MIND WAS WANDERING.

SURE, YOU MUSTA BEEN UP ALL NIGHT! WHY DON'T YOU GO GET SOME SHUT-EYE?

BUT AT THIS MOMENT, SLEEP IS THE LAST THING ON STEVE ROGERS' MIND!

A BIZARRE PRISON BREAK... CARRIED OFF BY A SMALL BAND OF MEN... AND A COUPLE OF THEM HAD FRENCH ACCENTS!

MAYBE I'M JUST PUNCHY FROM LACK OF SLEEP, BUT THIS IS STARTING TO SOUND LIKE THE KIND OF OPERATION BATROC WOULD BE BEHIND!

FROM PERSONAL EXPERIENCE-- AND THE INTERPOL FILES I'VE READ-- I KNOW SUCH A PRISON BREAK WOULD BE JUST ENOUGH OF A CHALLENGE TO APPEAL TO THAT CRAZY FRENCHMAN!

AND IF BATROC'S MIXED UP IN THIS--

--THEN *CAPTAIN AMERICA* IS DEFINITELY GETTING INVOLVED! NO NEED TO CALL THE AVENGERS IN ON THIS...

...AFTER ALL, THE ONLY THING I HAVE TO GO ON ARE SOME VAGUE HUNCHES! THE FIRST ORDER OF BUSINESS IS TO STOP IN AT THE DISTRICT ATTORNEY'S OFFICE!

IF D.A. TOWER IS INVESTIGATING THIS THING, HE MAY BE ABLE TO CHECK UP ON BATROC'S WHEREABOUTS!

I SURE HOPE NO ONE STUMBLES ACROSS MY STREET CLOTHES IN THAT JANITOR'S CLOSET WHERE I HID THEM!

AFTER ALL, WITH TODAY'S PRICES, I CAN'T AFFORD TO LOSE TOO MANY SUITS OR PORTFOLIOS!

SLAMM

WITH THAT ONE LAST, FLEETING THOUGHT TO HIS PERSONAL FORTUNES, CAP BOLTS ACROSS THE ROOFTOPS OF THE CITY--HIS EVERY MOVE-MENT CONCENTRATED TOWARDS CARRYING HIM TO HIS DESTINATION...

--A CERTAIN DOWNTOWN MUNICIPAL BUILDING...

IF NOTHING ELSE, HAVING A LITTLE TALK WITH TOWER SHOULD PUT MY MIND AT EASE!

I'M PROBABLY JUST GETTING PARANOID IN MY OLD AGE--

--BUT I CAN'T SHAKE THIS FEELING THAT BATROC'S BEHIND THIS. AND EXPERIENCE HAS TAUGHT ME TO GO WITH MY FEELINGS!

WH-WHAT'S HE DOING HERE? COULD HE HAVE FOUND OUT ABOUT THOSE KICK-BACKS?

≷WOW!≷

YEAH, IT'S REALLY HIM! WASN'T HE RUNNING FOR PRESIDENT OR SOMETHING*!

*SEE LAST ISSUE --J.S.

SHORTLY, IN THE OUTER OFFICES OF THE DISTRICT ATTORNEY...

SHIRLEY, I TELL YOU THIS JOB IS SUCH A DISAPPOINTMENT! I THOUGHT THAT BEING THE D.A.'S RECEPTIONIST WOULD BE SO GLAMOROUS!

NO, IT'S DEADLY DULL! THERE'S NEVER THE LEAST BIT OF EXCITEMENT!

PARDON ME, MISS--!

HAVE TO GO, SHIRL! SOMEONE JUST CAME IN! YEAH...LATER!

YES? MAY I HELP YOU?

≷OH!≷

I'D LIKE TO SEE THE D.A. --IF HE'S NOT BUSY!

I THINK I'M GONNA DIE!

AT THAT VERY MOMENT, JUST OFF THE COAST OF SANDY HOOK, NEW JERSEY -- A ROXXON L-N-G SUPER-TANKER THE QUEEN OF EGYPT, SPEEDS TOWARDS A NEW AND CONTROVERSIAL DOCKING FACILITY JUST OUTSIDE OF PERTH AMBOY...

... ITS CARGO: 50-THOUSAND TONS OF LIQUIFIED NATURAL GAS!

PEARSON?

AYE, SIR?

WHAT IN BLAZES IS THAT THING APPROACHING OFF THE PORT BOW?

OH... JUST A TUG PULLING A BARGE, SIR!

WELL, WARN THEM OFF! I DON'T WANT TO RISK A COLLISION! THE NEW YORK PAPERS ARE GIVING US THE DEVIL FROM THEIR FRONT PAGES, CALLING US A "FLOATING BOMB"--

--AND THE HOME OFFICE IS VERY ANXIOUS TO PROVE THEM WRONG... TO SHOW THAT THIS NEW TANKER AND FACILITY ARE SAFE.

WOO HOO HOO! AWRIGHT!

EH?

WHAT COULD POSSIBLY BE SO FASCINATING ABOUT A BARGE TO AN EXPERIENCED TANKER CREW?

OH. HAH-HA!

IT APPEARS THAT THE SKIPPER OF THAT TUG HAS BROUGHT A FRIEND ALONG! I MUST SAY HE HAS EXCELLENT TASTE!

NOW WHAT? SHE'S HOLDING UP SOME SORT OF SIGN... SAYING WE'VE BEEN...

SURPRISE! YOU'VE BEEN BOARDED!

... BOARDED?

SHE IS RIGHT, MON AM...

BUT ALLOW ME TO INTRODUCE MYSELF... I AM BATROC THE LEAPER!

PLEASE FORGIVE ME FOR KNOCKING OUT YOUR FIRST MATE, BUT I DID NOT WANT HIM TO SPOIL YOUR SURPRISE!

OH, YES... THAT GENTLEMAN ON THE DECK BELOW IS MY ASSOCIATE--

--MONSIEUR HYDE! I AM AFRAID HE DOES NOT THINK SO MUCH OF YOUR CREW!

AH, BUT I SEE YOU ARE CONFUSED! DO YOU WON-DER HOW WE GOT ABOARD YOUR SHIP.... OR SHOULD I SAY OUR SHIP? IT WAS QUITE SIMPLE--

--WE USED A LITTLE TWO-MAN SUBMARINE, AND CAME UP ON YOUR STARBOARD SIDE WHILE YOUR ATTENTION WAS DRAWN ELSEWHERE!

AND NOW, IF YOU WOULD PLEASE COME WITH ME--!

SOON, IN THE RADIO ROOM...

DO NOT SQUIRM, LITTLE MAN-- OTHER-WISE I MIGHT HAVE TO BREAK A FEW OF YOUR BONES!

'ALLO? SHIP-TO-SHORE OPERA-TOR? THIS IS THE QUEEN OF EGYPT CALLING! PLEASE CON-NECT ME WITH THE M'SIEUR PIERCE BENEDICT, THE DIRECTOR OF SEA-GOING OPERATIONS AT THE ROXXON CORPORATION IN NEW YORK!

I WILL WAIT.

WITHIN MINUTES, IN A PLUSH SUITE OF OFFICES AT ONE ROXXON PLAZA...

YOU WANT *WHAT*?! OR YOU'LL *WHAT*?! YOU... YOU CAN'T BE SERIOUG!

GOOD LORD, MAN, THAT'S UNTHINKABLE! THE LOSS OF LIFE ALONE WOULD BE MONSTROUS!

A BILLION DOLLARS RANSOM?! BUT WE CAN'T COME UP WITH THAT MUCH IN SO SHORT A TIME!

THIS IS HYDE SPEAKING, BENEDICT! DON'T GIVE ME ANY EXCUSES! YOUR BOARD OF DIRECTORS CONTROLS SEVERAL MAJOR MANHATTAN BANKS! YOU CAN RAISE THE MONEY!

NOW LISTEN GOOD! MY PARTNER AND I ARE SAILING THIS FLOATING POWDER-KEG OF YOURS RIGHT INTO THE MIDDLE OF NEW YORK HARBOR! IF WE DON'T RECEIVE OUR RANSOM IN TIME--

--WE BLOW UP THIS TANKER... AND ALL OF NEW YORK WITH IT!!

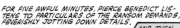

FOR FIVE AWFUL MINUTES, PIERCE BENEDICT LISTENS TO PARTICULARS OF THE RANSOM DEMANDS, FEVERISHLY JOTTING DOWN DETAILS.

HIS VOICE CHOKING WITH EQUAL PARTS OF FEAR AND RAGE, HE HURRIEDLY PLACES ANOTHER CALL...

LOOK, BLAST IT, I DON'T CARE IF HE'S IN A MEETING! I HAVE TO SPEAK WITH THE DISTRICT ATTORNEY NOW! THIS IS AN EMERGENCY!

AND SO...

YES, THIS IS BLAKE TOWER.

WHAT?!? YOU'RE SERIOUS?

CAP, YOUR HUNCH WAS RIGHT! BATROC IS INVOLVED... BUT IT'S MUCH WORSE THAN WE THOUGHT!

YES, GO ON, BENEDICT... WHAT ARE THEIR DEMANDS? HOW MUCH? UH HUH... AND THEY WANT A HOSTAGE AS WELL? THEY WANT WHO? YES, I'M SURE WE CAN GET HIM... I KNOW WE CAN!

SEVERAL HOURS LATER, THE QUEEN OF EGYPT SAILS PLACIDLY UNDER THE VERRAZANO NARROWS BRIDGE--

--ENTERING A NEW YORK HARBOR WHICH IS STRANGELY BEREFT OF ALL OTHER SEA-GOING TRAFFIC!

THERE, BATROC-- YOU SEE? THE ENTIRE HARBOR HAS BEEN CLEARED AS PER OUR ORDERS... THE ONLY THING AFLOAT OUT THERE IS THE RANSOM BARGE!

I TOLD YOU THAT ROXXON COULD RAISE THE MONEY!

YOU WERE RIGHT ONCE AGAIN, MON AMI! SOON, ALL OF THAT LOVELY OIL MONEY SHALL BE OURS! AND LOOK...

"... THEY HAVE EVEN SUPPLIED THE HOSTAGE WE ASKED FOR!"

I WOULD NEVER HAVE AGREED TO THIS, IF THE CITY WEREN'T IN THE GRAVEST OF DANGER!

THAT TANKER HAS THE EXPLOSIVE POTENTIAL OF A SMALL NUCLEAR BOMB... THE SLIGHTEST SPARK MIGHT SET IT OFF! I COULDN'T REFUSE ANY ROLE WHICH MIGHT SAVE THE LIVES OF TEN MILLION PEOPLE!

BUT I STILL DON'T LIKE THIS! AND WHY... WHY DID HYDE ASK FOR ME SPECIFICALLY AS A HOSTAGE? WHAT DO HE AND BATROC HAVE PLANNED?

EVER-SO-GINGERLY, THE MAMMOTH TANKER IS BROUGHT ALONGSIDE THE TINY BARGE...

HE'S TIED UP, ALL RIGHT! EVERY-THING'S CLEAR!

THEN... IT HAS BEEN A LONG TIME SINCE LAST WE MET, EH?

SO, MON CAPITAINE--

NOT LONG ENOUGH, BATROC!

MON VIEUX, YOU CUT ME TO THE QUICK!

DEAL WITH HIM LATER, BATROC! LET'S INSPECT THE BOOTY FIRST!

YES, IT'S ALL HERE... GOLD, PLATINUM, PRECIOUS METALS, LARGE PILES OF NON-SEQUENTIALLY-NUMBERED DOLLARS! WE'RE WEALTHY, BATROC!

I'D SAY WE CAN EVEN AFFORD TO HAVE SOME... FUN WITH OUR HOSTAGE! YOU FIRST, BATROC... AFTER ALL, HE WAS YOUR IDEA!

BATROC WANTED ME AS A HOSTAGE? ODD... BUT I DON'T HAVE TIME TO WONDER WHY JUST NOW!

SHIFTING HIS WEIGHT SLIGHTLY, CAP STEPS DOWN HARD ON A CERTAIN BOARD IN THE DECK AT HIS FEET...

CREAK

...TRIGGERING A SUDDEN, UNEXPECTED RELEASE OF KNOCK-OUT GAS!

NOM DÚN CHIEN! IT IS A TRICK!

BUT BATROC'S CHOKED WARNING COMES TOO LATE FOR HIS UNDERLINGS!

SNAP

I HATE USING SOME-THING AS UNDERHANDED AS THIS, BUT UNDER THE CIRCUMSTANCES, IT'S BEST TO TAKE OUT THESE GOONS AS QUICKLY AS POSSIBLE!

THE GAS WILL DISSIPATE IN A MINUTE... IN THE MEAN-TIME, THESE NOSE FILTERS SHOULD KEEP ME FROM BEING AFFECTED!

SACRE BLEU! YOUR TREACHEROUS GASES WILL NOT STOP THE GREAT BATROC!

NON! NOT THAT ACCURSED SHIELD OF YOURS AGAIN! I DID NOT EVEN SEE YOU GRAB IT UP! HOW COULD YOU POSSIBLY HAVE HAD TIME--?

WELL, BATROC--EITHER I'M GETTING FASTER, OR YOU'RE GETTING SLOWER!

AND BY THE WAY...DON'T TALK TO ME ABOUT TREACHERY, MISTER!

BONG

THE OLD BATROC I KNEW MIGHT HAVE BEEN A MERCENARY, BUT HE NEVER TRIED TO EXTORT MONEY BY THREATENING THE LIVES OF TEN MILLION PEOPLE!

THE BATROC I KNEW ONCE SAID, "MEN WITHOUT HONOR DESERVE NO MERCY!"

THAM

KNOW WHAT I MEAN?

NOW... WHERE'S THAT PARTNER OF YOURS?

RIGHT, HERE!

ALL RIGHT, LET'S GET THIS OVER WITH FAST! I SEEM TO REMEMBER YOU HAVING A GLASS JAW, HYDE!

THE LAST TIME WE FOUGHT, A GOOD RIGHT CROSS PUT YOU OUT OF ACTION! *

*CAP #152--JIM.

VERY GOOD, CAPTAIN! YOUR MEMORY IS EXCELLENT, EVEN IF YOUR REASONING IS FAULTY! YOU SEE, I WAS BUT A SHADOW OF MYSELF WHEN WE BATTLED BEFORE!

THAT IS NOT THE CASE TODAY!

EH?

THAT IS NOT THE CASE AT ALL! HA-HA-HA-HA-HAH!!

KRAK

SURPRISED BY HYDE'S RESILIENCE, CAPTAIN AMERICA--HIS REFLEXES DULLED FROM LACK OF SLEEP--FALLS BEFORE HYDE'S BLUDGEONING ATTACK!

WHUMP

WHUUD

MON DIEU! HYDE CAUGHT HIM OFF-GUARD... I DO NOT BELIEVE IT!

NON, HYDE, NON! DO YOU WANT TO KILL HIM ?!

YES! I THINK I DO!

BUT... SURELY THERE MUST BE SOME BETTER WAY! YOU ARE MR. HYDE! YOU DON'T HAVE TO PUMMEL HIM LIKE SOME COMMON THUG!

YES... YOU'RE RIGHT! THERE IS A BETTER WAY... AND THE MEANS OF CARRYING IT OUT ARE RIGHT AT HAND!

[99]

FOR CAPTAIN AMERICA, TIME CEASES TO HAVE MEANING. THERE IS ONLY A THICK, ALL-ENCOMPASSING DARKNESS, NUMBING HIS BRAIN... A DARKNESS WHICH MELTS AWAY VERY, VERY SLOWLY.

UNNGHH! I... CERTAINLY MISJUDGED HYDE'S MIGHT! HE'S MUCH MORE POWERFUL THAN THE LAST TIME WE FOUGHT... I DIDN'T EXPECT THAT!

WELL, HELLO, CAPTAIN! WELCOME BACK TO THE LIVING... FOR NOW!

EH?

WHAT THE DEVIL?!

YOU MAKE A MOST COLORFUL FIGUREHEAD, CAPTAIN! NO, DON'T TRY TO BREAK FREE... YOU'LL FIND IT QUITE IMPOSSIBLE TO SNAP THOSE CHAINS!

BUT DON'T FEEL TOO BAD... LOOK ON THE BRIGHT SIDE! YOU'LL HAVE A RINGSIDE SEAT WHEN I RETURN THIS TANKER--

--BY RAMMING IT... FULL SPEED... INTO THE DOCKS OF NEW YORK!!

AND BENEATH THE METAL HULL AT CAP'S BACK, FIFTY THOUSAND TONS OF LIQUIFIED NATURAL GAS SLOSH ABOUT IN THEIR TANKS, STRAINING TO BURST FREE IN A HOLOCAUST OF FLAME AND DEATH!

IS NEW YORK BURNING? FIND OUT NEXT ISSUE IN... COLD FIRE!!

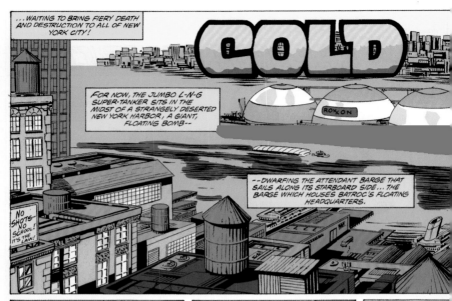

...WAITING TO BRING FIERY DEATH AND DESTRUCTION TO ALL OF NEW YORK CITY!

COLD

FOR NOW, THE JUMBO L-N-G SUPER-TANKER SITS IN THE MIDST OF A STRANGELY DESERTED NEW YORK HARBOR, A GIANT, FLOATING BOMB--

ROXXON

--DWARFING THE ATTENDANT BARGE THAT SAILS ALONG ITS STARBOARD SIDE... THE BARGE WHICH HOUSES BATROC'S FLOATING HEADQUARTERS.

NO SHOTS-- NO SCHOOL-- IT'S THE LAW!

BUT BEFORE THE TWO TAKE TO FLIGHT...

THIS LITTLE TOY OF YOURS FASCINATES ME, CAPTAIN! I THINK I'LL BREAK IT BEFORE I DEPART.

...AND YOU AND THE SHIP ARE BLOWN SKY-HIGH!

YOU MEAN YOU'LL *TRY*, HYDE! BETTER MEN THAN YOU HAVE FAILED!

HE SPEAKS THE TRUTH, HYDE! NOTHING SEEMS TO AFFECT HIS SHIELD!

NONSENSE! IT CAN'T... RESIST...ME! A PIECE OF METAL THIS SIZE... CAN'T... ≥UNGH≥... POSSIBLY--! I'VE... ≥UNGH≥ FOUGHT... ≥UNGH≥...THOR! I...I...

...I CAN'T.

BLAST!

UNABLE TO EVEN BEND THE MIGHTY SHIELD, HYDE HURLS IT OVER THE TANKER'S PORT SIDE--

2

FIRE!

HA-HAH-HA!

LESS THAN 24-HOURS AGO, BATROC USED THAT BARGE TO FREE HYDE FROM THE RYKER'S ISLAND PRISON COMPLEX. *

AND NOW, IT STANDS READY TO TRANSPORT THE DUO AND THEIR ILL-GOTTEN RANSOM TO SAFETY.

* LAST ISSUE. DON'T TELL US YOU MISSED IT! -- JIM.

--INADVERTANTLY LODGING IT DEEP IN THE SIDE OF A SECOND BARGE, WHERE BATROC'S MEN ARE FAITHFULLY GATHERING UP THE BILLION-DOLLAR RANSOM FOR TRANSFER.

KTUK

HUH?!

ROXXON

AND ON THE TANKER DECK...

I WAS A FOOL TO WASTE MY TIME ON THAT GAUDY TRINKET! COME, BATROC--WE STILL HAVE MUCH TO DO... ON THE BRIDGE!

QUEEN OF EGYPT

AS YOU SAY, MON AMI...

THERE IS MUCH WE STILL MUST DO!

UNNOTICED BY HYDE, BATROC NONCHALANTLY GIVES A GENTLE KICK TO THE PORT-SIDE ANCHOR CHAIN RELEASE--

③

...WITH SUDDEN CONSEQUENCES!

WHAT?! THERE'S SUDDENLY SLACK ON ONE OF MY CHAINS! IF ONLY IT'LL KEEP UP--!

NO GOOD! THE RATCHET-LOCK HAS KICKED BACK IN! ALL I GOT WAS A COUPLE EXTRA FEET OF CHAIN!

I GUESS I'LL HAVE TO MAKE THAT DO!

PULLING HIMSELF OVER TO THE STARBOARD SIDE, CAP BEGINS A PAINFUL MANEUVER...

GOT TO SCRAPE THE LINKS ACROSS THE BOW... AND TRY TO WEAKEN ONE OF THEM!

FOR LONG, AGONIZING MINUTES, CAP STRAINS TO HOLD HIMSELF IN PLACE AND WORK AT HIS BONDS. AND THEN...

THAT ONE LINK LOOKS LIKE IT MIGHT BE READY TO...

...GIVE!

GOOD! THE WELD GAVE! NOW... IF... I CAN JUST BEND IT ENOUGH!

COME ON, BLAST YOU-- BEND! BEND!

It BENDS...

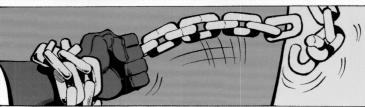

...AND WITH A GRATEFUL SIGH OF RELIEF, CAP FLIPS THE CHAIN LOOSE FROM THE RUPTURED LINK. IN SECONDS, HE IS FREE OF ONE OF HIS BONDS!

4

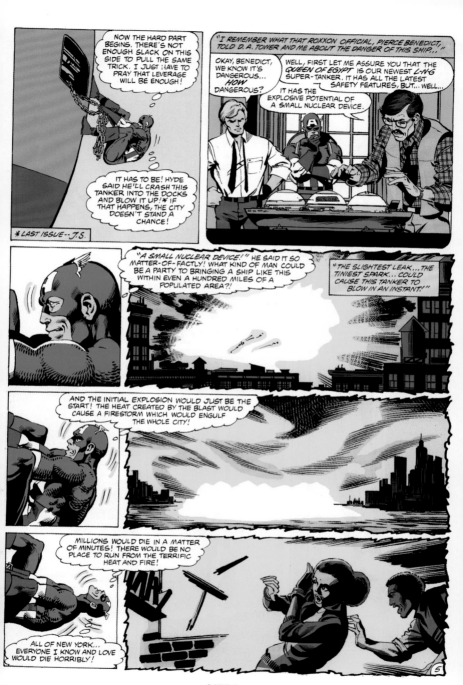

NO! THAT MUST NOT HAPPEN! I WON'T LET IT HAPPEN! I WON'T... I WON'T!!

FEAR AND OUTRAGE WELL UP IN THIS MAN'S SOUL... FEAR FOR THE LIVES OF MILLIONS OF NEW YORKERS... OUTRAGE AT BEING TRAPPED HERE, UNABLE TO DO MORE THAN STRAIN AND PULL!

EVERY MUSCLE, EVERY NERVE ENDING SCREAMS AS HE DESPERATELY TRIES TO BREAK FREE. THE CHAIN THAT BINDS HIM IS COLD, HARD STEEL...

... BY RIGHTS, IT SHOULD BE IMPOSSIBLE FOR HIM TO BREAK. BY RIGHTS, HE SHOULD GIVE UP.

BUT CAPTAIN AMERICA NEVER GIVES UP.

WITH EVERY BIT OF POWER IN HIS BODY, CAP GIVES A MIGHTY TUG! MIRACULOUSLY, THE CHAIN SEPARATES!

SN**AP**

#THUNK

AND THEN... TRAGEDY!

STUNNED, THE AVENGER PLUMMETS FROM THE BOW OF THE HUGE SUPER-TANKER...

...LIKE LEGENDARY ICARUS, FALLING FROM THE HEAVENS!

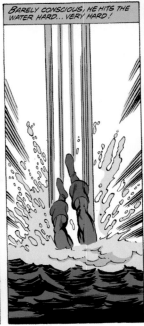

BARELY CONSCIOUS, HE HITS THE WATER HARD... VERY HARD!

AND IN SECONDS, THE ONE MAN WHO MIGHT POSSIBLY BE ABLE TO SAVE NEW YORK FROM TOTAL DESTRUCTION SINKS BENEATH THE WAVES...

...JUST LIKE A STONE!

6

MEANWHILE, ON THE BRIDGE OF THE MAMMOTH TANKER...

YES, BATROC, AS AN...ASSOCIATE, YOU HAVE BEEN MOST HELPFUL IN THIS OPERATION. AND OF COURSE, YOUR HOSTAGE CHOICE WAS A STROKE OF GENIUS... I COULDN'T HAVE DONE BETTER MYSELF!

AH...YES, I THOUGHT YOU WOULD LIKE IT.

THE *PIG!* IT IS BAD ENOUGH THAT HYDE TRICKED ME INTO WORKING WITH HIM, * BUT HE DOES NOT EVEN CONSIDER ME A FULL PARTNER!

*LAST ISSUE--JIM.

I STILL REMEMBER THE DEFEAT CAPTAIN AMERICA HANDED ME IN OUR PREVIOUS ENCOUNTER. HAVING HIM AT MY MERCY NOW IS MOST SATISFYING!

YES, I REMEMBER...

"...AT THE TIME, I HAD BEEN MR. HYDE FOR TOO LONG WITHOUT RE-NEWING THE CHEMICALS WHICH GIVE ME MY POWER.

"WHEN I FIRST FOUGHT CAPTAIN AMERICA, MY STRENGTH WAS JUST A FRACTION OF MY TRUE MIGHT. HE EASILY BESTED ME. *

*CAP #152--JIM

"AFTER THAT IGNOMINIOUS DEFEAT, HE JUST LEFT ME THERE, TIED UP WITH THAT FOOL, THE SCORPION... A PRISONER FOR THE POLICE TO FIND!

"BUT, AS I REGAINED CONSCIOUS-NESS, I REVERTED TO MY HUMAN FORM. ONCE AGAIN, I WAS DR. CALVIN ZABO! I EASILY SLIPPED FROM THE ROPES, LEAVING THE SCORPION FOR THE POLICE!

"I WAS ANGRY. I WANTED VENGEANCE ON THAT BLASTED AVENGER! BUT FOR THAT--

"--I NEEDED CERTAIN CHEMICALS TO DUPLICATE MY HYDE-FORMULA. FOOLISHLY, I BROKE INTO A NEARBY PHARMACY, AND I WAS CAUGHT IN THE ACT!

"LACKING THE FUNDS TO HIRE THE PROPER LAWYERS, I WAS TRIED AND CONVICTED, AND SO, CALVIN ZABO SPENT SIX MONTHS IN PRISON.

"SIX MONTHS DURING WHICH MY FORMER PARTNER, THE COBRA, BOUNCED IN AND OUT OF PRISONS AS A MEMBER OF THE SERPENT SQUAD!" *

*SEE CAP #163 & #180-182--JIM

⑦

[109]

EVEN WHEN I REJOINED THE COBRA, HE BETRAYED ME! HE LEFT ME TO ROT IN RYKER'S ISLAND,* AND HE IS THE SOLE BEING WHO KNOWS I AM CALVIN ZABO!

YOU ARE STRANGELY QUIET, M'SIEUR.

I WAS THINKING OF A MAN I WAS ONCE FOOLISH ENOUGH TO TRUST, BATROC... A MAN WHO MUST SUFFER FOR HIS TREACHERY!

*SEE SPECTACULAR SPIDER-MAN #46—J.

LOOK OUT THERE, BATROC... NEW YORK! JUST A FEW NIGHTS AGO, THE COBRA FOUGHT SPIDER-MAN OUT THERE!

I KNOW, COBRA...HE'S A CREATURE OF HABIT. HE'LL STILL BE HOLED UP IN THE CITY SOMEWHERE!

ALL I HAVE TO DO IS SET THESE CONTROLS... LET THIS TANKER CRASH INTO THE DOCKS... AND THE EXPLOSION WILL DO THE REST!

NO MORE NEW YORK... NO MORE COBRA!

YOU CANNOT BE SERIOUS! THAT WAS JUST A THREAT... A BLUFF TO GET THE MONEY FROM ROXXON AND BEDEVIL THE CAPTAIN!

YOU SHOULD KNOW ME BETTER BY NOW, BATROC! I AM QUITE SERIOUS!

AND YOU SHOULD KNOW BETTER, MONSIEUR, THAN TO TURN YOUR BACK ON BATROC!

SIGNAL YOUR MEN TO FINISH LOADING THE RANSOM AND CLEAR OUT OF THE HARBOR, WE'LL ESCAPE IN MY MINI-SUB!

NON! TAKING MONEY FROM A THIEVING OIL CARTEL LIKE ROXXON IS ONE THING, BUT MASS MURDER IS QUITE A DIFFERENT MATTER! BATROC SHALL HAVE NO PART OF IT!

JUST LAST NIGHT, BATROC ATTACKED HYDE WITH A SIMILAR KICK... A KICK MEANT TO PARALYZE. IT FAILED.

KTAM

TODAY, THE KICK IS DEADLIER... MEANT TO KILL!

8

IT ALSO FAILS!

KRESH

SACRE BLEU!

FOOL! DIDN'T YOU LEARN ANYTHING YESTERDAY?!

HYDE IS YOUR BETTER! HYDE WILL *ALWAYS* BE YOUR BETTER!

I STILL CANNOT BELIEVE THE SPEED HE POSSESSES! BUT SPEED AND STRENGTH ALONE DO NOT BRING VICTORY!

I DO NOT BELITTLE YOUR POWER, MONSIEUR--

KRAK

BUT EVEN THE MIGHTIEST CAN BE CAUGHT OFF GUARD!

AND NOW, WE SHALL SEE WHO IS TRULY THE SUPERIOR FIGHTER!

THE GLOVES ARE OFF, *N'EST-CE PAS?*

9

AND, SURE ENOUGH...

GREAT SCOTT! HYDE HAS BATROC ON THE ROPES! HE'S CRUSHING THE LIFE OUT OF HIM!

HYDE! NO!

STRANGE! FOR A MOMENT THERE, I THOUGHT I HEARD CAPTAIN AMERICA'S VOICE!

BUT THAT'S IMPOSSIBLE, ISN'T IT, BATROC? THE GOOD CAPTAIN IS AS HELPLESS AS YOU ARE!

S-S-STOP!

STOP? WHY CERTAINLY... AS SOON AS I'VE BROKEN YOU IN TWO! I THINK...AARRGHH!

MY ARM!

THE MAN SAID "STOP" HYDE--

-- THAT SEEMS LIKE A WISE DECISION!

YOU... FREE?! BUT HOW?!

PERHAPS HE HAD SOME HELP, NON?

MERCI, CAPITAN... THAT IS ONE I OWE YOU!

BAH! IT DOESN'T MATTER HOW YOU GOT FREE! I BEAT YOU UNCONCSIOUS AND CHAINED YOU BEFORE... I CAN DO IT AGAIN!

11

[113]

YEP, I'LL ADMIT THAT YOU CERTAINLY TOOK ME BY SURPRISE EARLIER, HYDE! BUT I'M ON MY GUARD NOW-- YOU WON'T TAKE ME THE SAME WAY TWICE!

FOOL! YOU CANNOT EVADE ME FOR LONG! YOU ARE JUST AN ORDINARY MAN... BUT I AM HYDE! *HYDE!*

WELL, THEN HERE'S AN INTERESTING LESSON FOR YOU...."*NEVER UNDERESTIMATE THE ORDINARY MAN!*"

THWAK

VERY TRUE, *MON AMI!* AND IS IT NOT ALSO A CUSTOM OF YOUR COUNTRYMEN TO BAND TOGETHER TO FIGHT THE COMMON EVIL?

BATROC! SO YOU STILL WANT A PART OF THIS FIGHT?

KRUK

BUT OF COURSE! YOU DID NOT THINK I WAS WILLING TO LET THIS MADMAN EXTERMINATE NEW YORK, DID YOU? WHY DID YOU THINK I ASKED FOR YOU AS OUR HOSTAGE?

WHUUFF!

THAT QUESTION *HAD* ENTERED MY MIND!

I NEVER TRUSTED HYDE FOR A MOMENT, AND I FEARED WHAT HE MIGHT TRY. BUT I KNEW THAT IF ANYONE COULD FIND A WAY TO STOP HIM, IT WAS YOU.

SO-- VOILA! I CONNIVED TO HAVE YOU BROUGHT HERE!

BATROC, THE NEXT TIME YOU NEED MY HELP AGAINST HYDE, GIVE ME A LITTLE WARNING FIRST!

RIGHT NOW, IT LOOKS LIKE EVERYTHING DEPENDS ON US!

YOU INSIGNIFICANT IDIOTS! HYDE HAS THE STRENGTH OF A DOZEN MEN!

THEN WE SHALL HAVE TO HIT YOU SEVERAL TIMES, *NON?*

NO! YOU ARE NOTHING TO ME!

HE'S NOT BLUFFING! OUR ONLY HOPE IS TO KEEP HIM OFF-BALANCE--

--AND TRY TO WEAR HIM DOWN!

FOR TOO LONG HYDE HAS ALLIED HIMSELF WITH WEAKLINGS AND TRAITORS... BUT NO MORE! HYDE NEEDS NO ONE BUT HIMSELF!

THANG

HEADS UP, BATROC! COMING YOUR WAY!

BACK AND FORTH ACROSS THE DECKS OF THE SUPER-TANKER, CAP AND BATROC STRIKE OUT AT HYDE-- ALWAYS TRYING TO MANEUVER HIM AWAY FROM THE VOLATILE *L-N-G* TANKS.

LIKE A WELL-HONED MACHINE, THEY ATTACK AGAIN AND AGAIN--

-- AND AGAIN!

KRUD

BUT THEN...

BATROC-- *LOOK OUT!*

HAH! I KNEW ONE OF YOU WOULD GET TOO CLOSE EVENTUALLY!

SPAM

13

WITH A LOOK OF MERCILESS GLEE ON HIS FACE, HYDE MOVES IN, READY TO DELIVER A KILLING BLOW! BUT BEFORE HE CAN...

NO! KEEP AWAY FROM HIM!

COME ON, MISTER, STAY ON YOUR FEET! PULL YOURSELF TOGETHER--I'LL HANDLE HYDE!

UNNGH!

YOU THINK YOU CAN STAND UP TO ME WITH THAT SHIELD, DO YOU? VERY WELL, HYDE SHALL USE A WEAPON, TOO!

THE WORDS SPEW FROM HYDE'S MOUTH IN A CHOKING, BRUTAL SNARL-- HIS MIND NOW ALL-BUT-OVERWHELMED BY HIS CONSUMING HATRED!

ADDLED BY HIS RAGE, HE RIPS FREE THE NEAREST OBJECT...

--AND IS INUNDATED BY A HIGH-PRESSURE STREAM OF LIQUIFIED NATURAL GAS!

GOOD LORD!

ALMOST INSTANTLY, AN ELABORATE EMERGENCY VALVE-SYSTEM SHUTS DOWN THE LEAK--BUT NOT BEFORE THE SUB-ZERO LIQUID FREEZES THE VERY WATER VAPOR AROUND HYDE!

H-HE'S STILL MOVING! HE'S STILL ALIVE UNDER ALL OF THAT!

14

ENCASED IN THE ICY SUBSTANCE, HYDE'S MONSTROUS FORM SLIPS AWAY FROM CAP'S GRASP, TUMBLING BACKWARD OVER THE SIDE OF THE TANKER...

HYDE!

JUST MINUTES AGO, HYDE THREATENED THE LIVES OF EVERY MAN, WOMAN AND CHILD IN NEW YORK CITY!

NOW, HE HIMSELF IS CAUGHT UP IN A DEATH-TRAP CREATED BY HIS OWN SAVAGE RAGE!

SPLOOSH

BUT CAPTAIN AMERICA DOES NOT HESITATE FOR A MOMENT. A LIFE IS IN DANGER... HE ACTS!

DESPERATELY, HE DIVES AFTER HYDE-- AGAIN AND AGAIN! BUT...

IT'S NO USE! THE HARBOR WATER IS TOO MURKY, I'VE LOST HIM!

I CAN'T FIND HIM, BATROC! WE'D BETTER RADIO THE HARBOR PATROL!

BATROC?

BUT THE WILY LEAPER IS NO LONGER ABOARD THE TANKER, HE IS ALREADY SEVERAL HUNDRED YARDS AWAY!

BLOOT BLOOT

15

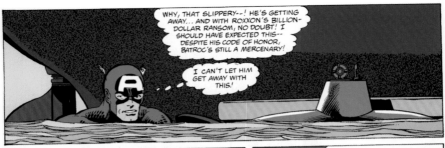

WHY, THAT SLIPPERY--! HE'S GETTING AWAY... AND WITH ROXXON'S BILLION-DOLLAR RANSOM, NO DOUBT! I SHOULD HAVE EXPECTED THIS-- DESPITE HIS CODE OF HONOR, BATROC'S STILL A MERCENARY!

I CAN'T LET HIM GET AWAY WITH THIS!

AND, ABOARD THE DECEPTIVELY INNOCENT-LOOKING BARGE...

IT...IT IS SO 'EAVY!

BUT OF COURSE, MONIQUE! GOLD IS HARDLY LIGHT!

ROXXON

MY LITTLE PLAN WORKED OUT WELL, DID IT NOT, *MA CHERIE?* NEW YORK IS STILL SAFE, MONSIEUR HYDE IS DEFEATED, AND WE HAVE ALL THIS LOVELY MONEY!

COME....LET US CELEBRATE!

BUT THEN...

BOOOM

NOM DU CHIEN!

MON DIEU!! DON'T TELL ME THAT THE TANKER BLEW UP AFTER ALL!

NON, WHAT AM I THINKING? THE EXPLOSION WOULD HAVE BEEN MUCH WORSE!

RACING UP THE STAIRS FROM HIS PRIVATE QUARTERS, DEEP WITHIN THE BARGE, BATROC SOON CONFRONTS THE PROBLEM...

OH, NO!

16

NEXT ISSUE: SHOULD OLD ACQUAINTANCE BE FORGOT

BACK IN THE DAWNING DAYS OF WORLD WAR TWO... WHEN DR. ERSKINE'S SUPER-SOLDIER SERUM TRANSFORMED FRAIL STEVE ROGERS INTO THE LIVING DYNAMO KNOWN AS **CAPTAIN AMERICA**, A LIFE WAS CHANGED FOR ALL TIME! THE YOUTHFUL HERO WAS SUDDENLY THRUST INTO A FOUR-YEAR CAREER OF ALMOST CONSTANT ACTION--

-- AND, FOR ALL INTENTS AND PURPOSES, STEVE ROGERS CEASED TO EXIST. HE BECAME LITTLE MORE THAN AN IDENTITY FOR CAPTAIN AMERICA TO FALL BACK ON.

FOR THE NEWLY-INDUCTED PRIVATE ROGERS, LIFE VARIED FROM THE FANTASTIC ADVENTURES OF CAPTAIN AMERICA... TO THE BORING ROUTINE OF BOOT CAMP.

THROWN INTO SUSPENDED ANIMATION BY A FREAK ACCIDENT AT WAR'S END, CAP WAS FOUND AND REVIVED DECADES LATER BY THE MIGHTY AVENGERS. AMERICA'S SUPER-SOLDIER LIVED AGAIN!

BUT, AS BEFORE, STEVE ROGERS WAS LITTLE MORE THAN A CIPHER. WHEN NOT ON A MISSION WITH THE AVENGERS, CAP FOUND HIMSELF WITH LITTLE TO DO. CLEARLY, SOMETHING HAD TO CHANGE!

FOR A SHORT TIME, CAP LED A SECOND LIFE AS A ROOKIE COP FOR THE NEW YORK POLICE DEPARTMENT, BUT WHILE THAT CAREER WAS SOME-WHAT SATISFYING FOR STEVE ROGERS, IT DIDN'T ALLOW HIM THE FLEXIBILITY NEEDED TO CONTINUE AS CAPTAIN AMERICA.

MACY'S

TODAY, HOWEVER, CAP HAS FINALLY FOUND A CAREER THAT ALLOWS ENOUGH TIME FOR A DOUBLE LIFE, AND ENOUGH INCOME TO PAY THE RENT.

MEET STEVE ROGERS,... FREE-LANCE COMMERCIAL ARTIST!

PUSH

DRAWING ON A NATIVE TALENT FOR ART, STEVE HAS AT LAST RETURNED TO LIFE... A LIFE OF FLEXIBLE HOURS... CREATIVE FULFILLMENT...

...AND DEADLINES!

THE APARTMENT OF STEVE ROGERS ESQ.

LOCATED AT 569 LEAMAN PLACE, IN THE VERY HEART OF HISTORIC BROOKLYN HEIGHTS, STEVE'S APARTMENT-&-STUDIO OCCUPIES THE TOP FLOOR OF A HANDSOME OLD FOUR-STORY BUILDING.

FINALLY, FOR ALL YOU BUDDING ARCHITECTS, HERE'S THE FLOORPLAN TO STEVE'S HUMBLE ABODE...

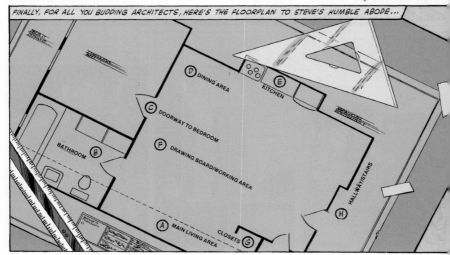

D DINING AREA

E KITCHEN

C DOORWAY TO BEDROOM

BATHROOM B

F DRAWING BOARD/WORKING AREA

HALLWAY/STAIRS H

A MAIN LIVING AREA

CLOSETS G

STEVE ROGERS' FRIENDS AND NEIGHBORS

ANNA KAPPLEBAUM... THE SURROGATE MOTHER OF THE OTHER TENANTS AT 569 LEAMAN PLACE. ANNA IS A SURVIVOR OF HITLER'S DEATH CAMPS. SHE LITTLE SUSPECTS THAT HANDSOME YOUNG STEVE ROGERS IS THE SAME MAN WHO--AS CAPTAIN AMERICA--SAVED HER LIFE DURING THE FINAL DAYS OF WORLD WAR TWO.

JOSHUA COOPER... ALSO KNOWN AS "THE COOP." A FORMER ARMY MEDIC, JOSH IS NOW A TEACHER, WORKING WITH CHILDREN WHO HAVE SEVERE LEARNING DISABILITIES. IT'S NOT AN EASY JOB, BUT JOSH WOULDN'T TRADE AN HOUR WITH HIS KIDS FOR ALL THE GOLD IN FORT KNOX.

MICHAEL FARREL... INVETERATE READER AND FULL-TIME FIREMAN. A GRADUATE OF THREE DIFFERENT COLLEGES, AND A HOLDER OF A HALF-DOZEN OR SO DEGREES, MIKE ALWAYS WANTED TO BE A FIREMAN. TO HIS CREDIT, HE'S ONE OF THE BEST.

BERNADETTE ROSENTHAL... "BERNIE" TO HER FRIENDS. MS. ROSENTHAL IS ONE OF THE MOST TALENTED GLASS BLOWERS IN THE NEW YORK METROPLEX. IT IS ALSO RUMORED THAT SHE HAS MORE THAN A PASSING INTEREST IN STEVE ROGERS.

CAPTAIN AMERICA'S PARTNERS AGAINST CRIME

COLONEL NICHOLAS FURY & AGENT TIMOTHY ALOYSIUS CADWALLADER DUGAN (A.K.A. DUM-DUM)... OF THE SUPREME HEADQUARTERS INTERNATIONAL ESPIONAGE LAW-ENFORCEMENT DIVISION.

THE DIRECTOR OF THE FREE WORLD'S GREATEST SPY-AGENCY AND HIS TOP AGENT HAVE OFTEN FOUGHT ALONGSIDE CAP IN HIS BATTLES AGAINST THE ENEMIES OF FREEDOM!

SAM WILSON THE FALCON...AND MS. LEILA TAYLOR.

CAP'S FORMER PARTNER-- AND ONE-TIME FELLOW AVENGER --IS NOW OPERATING ON HIS OWN. (ACTUALLY, WE'RE NOT SURE JUST WHAT SAM AND HIS LADY ARE UP TO RIGHT NOW, BUT WE DOUBT THEY'LL STAY OUT OF THE PICTURE FOR LONG!)

JAMES BUCHANAN BARNES -- A.K.A. BUCKY

S.H.I.E.L.D. AGENT 13-- SHARON CARTER

THE WAR AGAINST INJUSTICE IS NOT AN EASY ONE... LIKE ANY WAR, IT HAS ITS CASUALTIES. CAP'S FIRST PARTNER, BUCKY, AND THE LOVE OF HIS LIFE, SHARON CARTER, WERE TWO OF THOSE CASUALTIES. AND THOUGH THEY HAVE PASSED FROM THIS MORTAL EXISTENCE, THEY SHALL NEVER BE FORGOTTEN!

AND FINALLY, THERE ARE CAP'S TEAMMATES...THE AVENGERS!

CHICKEN!

DEAR ROGER,
IF YOU THINK I'M GOING TO DRAW ALL OF THE AVENGERS - EVERY SINGLE MEMBER AND ALL OF THE VARIOUS HANGERS-ON - IN THIS LITTLE SPACE, YOU CAN THINK AGAIN!

JOHN BYRNE

THANKS JOHN! -- JOE RUBINSTEIN

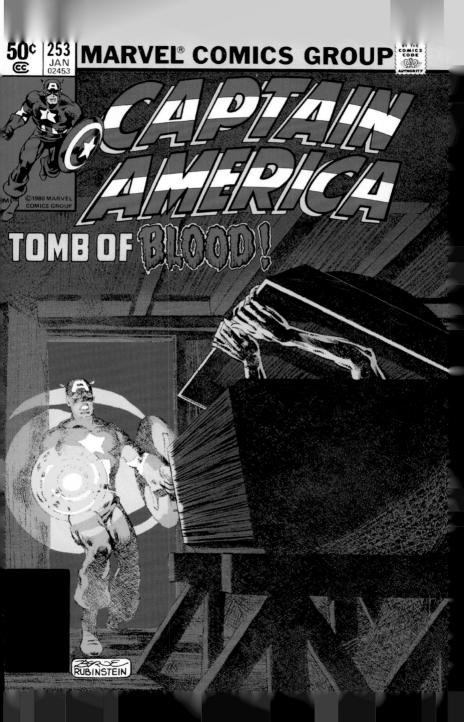

1940! As the world teetered on the brink of global war, frail *Steve Rogers* entered a secret laboratory and was transformed into the American *super-soldier!* For four thrilling years, he battled the Axis powers — until a freak stroke of fate threw him into *suspended animation.* When he awoke, he was a man decades out of his time! Since that fateful day, Steve Rogers has sought his destiny in this brave new world!

STan Lee PRESENTS: **CAPTAIN AMERICA!**

SHOULD OLD ACQUAINTANCE BE FORGOT

THE RAINS WASH DOWN ON THE SMALL BRITISH VILLAGE, NOT FAR FROM THE NORTH OF LONDON.

THEY ARE NOT CLEANSING RAINS...

OVER HERE, DOCTOR! LOOKS LIKE THE BLOODY SLASHER'S STRUCK AGAIN!

BLAST! THAT'S THE THIRD VICTIM IN LESS THAN A MONTH. WHEN... WHEN WILL IT ALL END?

ROGER STERN & JOHN BYRNE WRITER/CO-PLOTTERS/PENCILER | JOE RUBINSTEIN INKER

JIM NOVAK, LETTERER | BOB SHAREN, COLORIST

JIM SALICRUP, EDITOR | JIM SHOOTER, CHIEF

MMM... IT'S THE SLASHER'S WORK, ALL RIGHT. THE NECK WAS BROKEN... THROAT MUTILATED... AND I DOUBT THAT THERE'S AN OUNCE OF BLOOD LEFT IN HER.

POOR GIRL -- AT LEAST THE END MUST HAVE COME QUICKLY.

COR', DOCTOR... TO THINK THAT THERE'S A BLOODY MADMAN LIKE THE SLASHER RUNNIN' AROUND FREE! WHAT MANNER OF MAN KILLS AN INNOCENT WOMAN--

--AN' THEN DRAINS OFF 'ER BLOOD LIKE A SLAUGHTERHOUSE PIG?

A VERY... SICK ONE, CONSTABLE.

COME, HELP ME GET THE LASS'S BODY TO MY OFFICE. THEN, WE'D BEST INFORM HER LADYSHIP OF THIS!

MINUTES, LATER, AT A NEARBY MANOR HOUSE...

WE'RE SORRY ABOUT INTRUDIN' AT SUCH A BEASTLY HOUR, LADY CRICHTON--

--BUT YOU ASKED TO BE KEPT POSTED ON THIS SLASHER BUSINESS.

THAT'S QUITE ALL RIGHT, CONSTABLE--

--I HAD YET TO RETIRE FOR THE EVENING... AND I DARE SAY THAT I DOUBT I'LL GET ANY SLEEP THIS NIGHT!

SOMETHING MUST BE DONE BEFORE THE SLASHER CLAIMS ANOTHER VICTIM. I STILL HAVE SOME INFLUENCE WITH SCOTLAND YARD, YOU KNOW... I'LL BRING INSPECTOR SWEENEY IN ON THIS RIGHT OFF!

THAT'S VERY GOOD OF YOU, YOUR LADYSHIP!

OH, HOW-- MIGHT I ASK-- IS YOUR FATHER DOING?

FATHER IS AS WELL AS COULD BE EXPECTED, DOCTOR-- THANK YOU FOR ASKING. THAT MEDICATION YOU GAVE HIM SEEMS TO HAVE EASED HIS CHEST PAINS...

...THOUGH I'M AFRAID HE'S STILL AS STUBBORN AS EVER!

THE FOOLS!

I'VE TOLD THEM WHO THIS SLASHER IS, BUT THEY IGNORE ME! CAN'T THEY SEE THAT THE DEVIL HAS RETURNED AMONG US?

HE MUST BE STOPPED, BUT THERE'S NOT A MAN AMONG THEM WHO IS CAPABLE!

NO, THE ONLY MAN WHO CAN STOP THESE MURDERS IS AN OCEAN AWAY!

SIX TIME ZONES ACROSS THE WIDE ATLANTIC LIES **NEW YORK CITY**! IT IS A GREAT CITY... A WORLD CITY...

...BUT EVEN THE GREATEST CITIES HAVE THEIR SHARE OF HUMAN VERMIN.

C'MON, I KNOW YOU GOTTA HAVE MORE DOUGH THAN THAT! HAND IT OVER!

I HAFF ALREADY EMPTIED CASH REGISTER... THAT IS ALL I HAFF! VHAT MORE YOU VANT FROM ME.,. BLOOD?

IF THEY DO, THEY WON'T GET IT!

WITH A DESPERATE SUDDENNESS, THE ARMED ROBBER WHIRLS AND FIRES BOTH BARRELS OF HIS WEAPON AT THE BOLD FIGURE WHO DASHES THROUGH THE DOORWAY.

BUT, FAST AS THE GUNMAN IS, HIS ACTION IS MUCH TOO SLOW!

IT CAN'T BE! NO MAN CAN DODGE A SHOTGUN BLAST AT THIS RANGE!

MISTER, I WAS DODGING A LOT WORSE THAN THAT-- A LOT CLOSER THAN THAT-- BEFORE YOU WERE BORN!

THERE IS NO BRAGGADOCIO IN THE VOICE OF THE COLORFULLY CLAD MAN-- ONLY CALM CONFIDENCE-- AS HE TAKES OUT ONE OPPONENT AND TURNS TO CHASE AFTER THE SECOND...

'S CAPTAIN 'MERICA! I'VE 'EARD ABOUT 'IM MOST'A 'Y LIFE--

THAT FELLOW HAS A PRETTY GOOD HEAD START! STILL, I COULD EASILY CATCH HIM BEFORE HE REACHES THE END OF THE ALLEY--

--BUT I DON'T HAVE THE TIME TO WASTE RIGHT NOW! THIS WAY WILL BE FASTER!

CLANG

CLANG

--BUT I NEVER ACTUALLY THOUGHT HE WAS FOR REAL! I GOTTA GET OUTTA HERE!

POWERED BY NOTHING MORE THAN HIS GOOD RIGHT ARM, CAPTAIN AMERICA'S SHIELD RICOCHETS DOWN THE ALLEYWAY, SWIFTLY ARCING BACK IN ON THE FLEEING FELON.

:WHUUF!:

BLASTED THING KNOCKED THE WIND OUTTA ME. BUT *I* GOT IT NOW... AND HE DON'T.

OKAY, MAN... HOLD IT RIGHT THERE! I GOT A PIECE, SEE--AN' I'M NOT AFRAID TO USE IT!

I DON'T DOUBT THAT A BIT, SON. BUT I'M NOT AFRAID, EITHER.

I DIDN'T NEED MY SHIELD TO AVOID YOUR BUDDY'S SHOTGUN BLAST... AND I DON'T NEED IT NOW.

IF YOU WANT TO SHOOT ME-- GO AHEAD AND TRY. BUT REMEMBER THIS... A LOT OF MEN HAVE TRIED... A LOT OF MEN WHO'VE FAILED!

UNLESS YOU FEEL LIKE YOU WANT TO FAIL MORE THAN YOU ALREADY HAVE, I'D ADVISE YOU TO HAND THAT THING OVER!

FOR WHAT SEEMS TO BE AN ETERNITY, THE TREMBLING HOODLUM STARES UP INTO THE ALERT BLUE EYES OF THE COSTUMED MAN.

FEVERISHLY, HE WEIGHS THE ODDS. IT SHOULD BE IMPOSSIBLE FOR THE AVENGER TO KEEP FROM TAKING A BULLET, AS CLOSE AS HE IS.

BUT THIS IS CAPTAIN AMERICA HE FACES--

--AND CAPTAIN AMERICA, IT HAS BEEN SAID, DOES THE IMPOSSIBLE.

IN THE END, THERE IS ONLY ONE SANE RESPONSE.

H-H-HERE... TAKE IT!

I THINK IT WOULD BE BEST IF *YOU* TOOK THIS, SIR. THIS MAN WON'T BE GIVING YOU ANY MORE TROUBLE!

HOO-BOY! I BE BETTINK NOT! DAT ONE YOU HIT-- HE STILL IS OUT THE COLD! DAT VAS THE MOST AMAZINK TING I EVER SEE!

I CALLED THE POLICE... THEY BE HERE SOON!

FINE, THEN YOU WON'T BE NEEDING ME ANY LONGER! JUST KEEP AN EYE ON THAT ONE! OKAY?

FOR THE MAN WHO SAVES MINE LIFE... ANYTHING!

GOD BLESS YOU KEPTAIN!

ONE FAST FLIP UP A FIRE ESCAPE, AND CAPTAIN AMERICA IS ONCE AGAIN VAULTING OVER THE ROOF-TOPS OF THE CITY...

NORMALLY, I WOULD'VE WAITED AROUND FOR THE POLICE TO ARRIVE -- BUT THIS PARTICULAR EVENING --

--I HAVE A VERY IMPORTANT ENGAGEMENT, AND I'LL BE LATE FOR IT IF I DON'T HURRY!

AH, GOOD! THERE'S MY PORTFOLIO... RIGHT WHERE I LEFT IT!

HOPEFULLY, THERE WON'T BE ANY NEW EMERGENCIES CALLING FOR CAPTAIN AMERICA'S ATTENTION THIS EVENING --

-- BECAUSE IT'S ABOUT TIME THAT *STEVE ROGERS* ENJOYED A NIGHT ON THE TOWN!

A QUICK CHANGE OF CLOTHING, AND FREELANCE ARTIST STEVEN ROGERS SLIPS BACK DOWN INTO THE CITY STREETS --

--AND HEADS FOR A CERTAIN BROADWAY THEATRE, WHERE THE LOVELY BERNADETTE ROSENTHAL AWAITS...MORE OR LESS PATIENTLY!

I SHOULD HAVE KNOWN BETTER THAN TO EXPECT STEVE TO BE ON TIME!

HELLO, BERNIE-- SORRY I'M LATE. HAVE YOU BEEN WAITING LONG?

WELL, NOT LONG ENOUGH FOR MOSS TO GROW ON MY NORTH SIDE, STEVE. NO, YOU'RE NOT ALL THAT LATE...I THINK WE CAN STILL GET TO OUR SEATS BEFORE THE CURTAIN GOES UP.

THAT'S A RELIEF...

...I WAS AFRAID WE'D MISS THE OPENING NUMBER. AND I'VE BEEN LOOKING FORWARD TO SEEING THIS SHOW AGAIN FOR SOME TIME.

OH, YOU'VE SEEN IT BEFORE?

ONCE... YEARS AGO. THOUGH I DOUBT YOU'D BELIEVE ME IF I TOLD YOU THE YEAR WAS 1943!

HOURS LATER, AFTER AN EVENING OF RODGERS AND HAMMERSTEIN, STEVE AND BERNIE RETURN TO THEIR BROOKLYN HEIGHTS APARTMENT BUILDING...

COME ON--ADMIT IT, BERNIE! YOU KIDDED ME ABOUT WANTING TO SEE AN "OLD FOGEY'S MUSICAL"-- BUT YOU REALLY ENJOYED OKLAHOMA, DIDN'T YOU?

ALL RIGHT... IT WAS A KICK. BUT I STILL THINK OH, CALCUTTA WOULD HAVE BEEN MORE FUN.

YES...WELL, I DON'T THINK I'M QUITE READY FOR THAT JUST YET. CREAM WITH YOUR COFFEE?

PLEASE.

YOU KNOW, STEVE, YOU ARE A CONSTANT PUZZLE TO ME. YOU'RE BRIGHT... WITTY... BUT YOUR TASTES ARE SO... OLD-FASHIONED!

GUILTY AS CHARGED, BERNIE. I'M AFRAID I'M JUST AN INCURABLE NOSTALGIA BUFF. I'D RATHER LISTEN TO BIG BANDS THAN TO ROCK...

...AND RATHER WATCH AN OLD BOGART FILM THAN MOST CURRENT MOVIES.

WELL, I'LL AGREE THAT SOME OF THE OLDER MOVIES ARE AMONG THE BEST. DO YOU REMEMBER BOGEY AND LAUREN BACALL IN *TO HAVE AND HAVE NOT*?

SURE... ONE OF MY FAVORITES.

I ESPECIALLY LIKED THE SCENE WHERE BACALL SAID, "IF YOU NEED ME, STEVE... JUST WHISTLE. YOU KNOW HOW TO WHISTLE... DON'T YOU?"

UM-HMM. "YOU JUST PUT YOUR LIPS TOGETHER AND--!"

BRINNG

HELLO? WHO IS THIS?

JARVIS,* SIR. SORRY TO CALL SO LATE, BUT A CABLE JUST ARRIVED FOR YOU -- FOR CAPTAIN AMERICA, RATHER-- AT AVENGERS MANSION, AND I THINK IT COULD BE IMPORTANT.

YOU *THINK*--?

YES, SIR-- IT'S APPARENTLY IN SOME SORT OF CODE. ALL THE CABLE SAYS IS: "THE FAT'S IN THE FIRE... TIME TO WAVE THE FLAG, DISCREETLY... TALLY-HO!" AND IT'S SIGNED "FALSWORTH."

I SEE... THANK YOU.

*BUTLER TO THAT WORLD-FAMOUS SUPER-TEAM, THE AVENGERS -- J.

JARVIS WAS RIGHT... IT WAS IN CODE. ONE I HAVEN'T HEARD SINCE WORLD WAR TWO!

STEVE... WHAT WAS THAT ALL ABOUT?

BERNIE... SOMETHING'S COME UP. I HAVE TO GO TO ENGLAND RIGHT AWAY. IT'S... PERSONAL BUSINESS.

I DON'T KNOW HOW LONG I'LL BE GONE. I KNOW WE'D TALKED ABOUT GOING ON THAT OUTING THIS WEEKEND, BUT NOW--!

OH, THAT'S ALL RIGHT, STEVE. AN OLD BOY FRIEND OF MINE IS DUE IN TOWN THIS WEEK-END... I'LL BE FINE.

WELL, I'D BETTER LEAVE SO YOU CAN PACK! HAVE A GOOD TRIP!

SHORTLY...

IF ONLY I COULD HAVE TOLD HER... EXPLAIN HOW I'M NEEDED OVERSEAS!

BUT THE BURDEN... THE DUTY OF BEING CAPTAIN AMERICA IS SOMETHING I DARE NOT SHARE WITH HER... NOT YET.

AND, IN THE OUTER HALL...

WHY DID I LIE TO STEVE LIKE THAT? WAS IT JUST BECAUSE HE WOULDN'T CONFIDE IN ME HIS "PERSONAL BUSINESS"?

THAT BOY FRIEND STORY WAS SO CHILDISH. OH, WHAT'S THE MATTER WITH ME?

HOURS LATER, A SLEEK CONCORDE JETLINER STREAKS EASTWARD OVER THE NIGHT-DARKENED ATLANTIC..AT FASTER THAN THE SPEED OF SOUND...

I HADN'T REALIZED THE AIR-FARE WAS SO HIGH. MY TICKET JUST ABOUT EXHAUSTED THE CASH RESERVE I'D BUILT UP IN MY SAVINGS ACCOUNT.

I'D HAVE BORROWED AN AVENGERS' QUINJET, BUT THE CODED MESSAGE IN THAT CABLE SAID TO COME INCOGNITO --

--SO IT MADE MORE SENSE FOR STEVE ROGERS TO USE A COMMERCIAL FLIGHT.

IT'S BEEN A LONG TIME SINCE I WAS IN ENGLAND. I STILL REMEMBER THAT *FIRST* VISIT-- BACK IN 1942--WHEN LONDON BECAME THE BASE OF OPERATIONS--

"--FOR THE TEAM WINSTON CHURCHILL CALLED *THE INVADERS!* THE HUMAN TORCH, THE SUB-MARINER, AND I FORMED THE CORE OF THAT GROUP--

"--ALONG WITH THE TORCH'S FLAMING SIDEKICK, TORO, AND MY OWN PARTNER, BUCKY. FOR FOUR LONG YEARS, WE FOUGHT THE BIZARRE NAZI MENACES OF FORTRESS EUROPA.

"AND FOR MOST OF THOSE YEARS, WE WERE JOINED BY TWO DARING BRITISH HEROES... THE MIGHTY *UNION JACK*... AND LOVELY YOUNG JACQUELINE FALSWORTH, WHO BECAME THE FLEET-FOOTED *SPITFIRE!*"

MASTER MAN

THE BLUE BULLET

THE FACE

AGENT AXIS

ASBESTOS LADY

WARRIOR WOMAN

THE SCARLET SCARAB

AND, IN THE END, OUR EFFORTS HELPED BRING ABOUT THE DOWNFALL OF THE MADMAN HITLER AND HIS TWISTED THIRD REICH,

SIR, COULD YOU PLEASE FASTEN YOUR SEATBELT? WE'LL BE LANDING SOON.

EH? OH... CERTAINLY. PARDON ME. I GUESS I WAS ... DAYDREAMING.

SIR?

SOMETIMES... IT ALL *SEEMS* LIKE A DREAM.

SHORTLY, AT LONDON'S HEATHROW AIRPORT...

NOW FOR THE HARD PART... GETTING THROUGH CUSTOMS.

I'D RATHER NOT HAVE THAT INSPECTOR THROW OPEN MY SUITCASE AND LET EVERYONE SEE MY SHIELD INSIDE.

UNTIL I KNOW THE NATURE OF THE EMERGENCY THAT THE CABLE HAD HINTED AT, IT WOULD BE BEST IF CAPTAIN AMERICA KEPT A LOW PROFILE.

NEXT.

I'M IN A BIT OF A HURRY.

SURE, MATE-- EVERYBODY IS! LET'S SEE YOUR PASSPORT!

NOW... DO YOU HAVE ANYTHING TO...

AVENGERS PRIORITY CLEARANCE

...DECLARE?

UH... RIGHT YOU ARE, SIR! EVERYTHING'S IN ORDER-- HAVE A GOOD STAY, SIR!

NEXT! LET'S KEEP IT MOVING!

ONE LONG CAB RIDE LATER...

FALSWORTH MANOR... IT HASN'T CHANGED A BIT IN ALL THESE YEARS. I STILL RECALL THE EARLY STRATEGY SESSIONS THE INVADERS HELD HERE, WHEN THIS WAS OUR TEMPORARY HEADQUARTERS.

I WONDER WHAT SORT OF EMERGENCY COULD HAVE ARISEN THAT THE FALSWORTHS COULDN'T HANDLE THEMSELVES?

WELL, WHATEVER IT IS, I'LL SOON FIND OUT.

PARDON ME, MA'AM, BUT IS THE LORD OF THE MANOR ABOUT?

HE IS, BUT I DOUBT THAT--! STEVE? *STEVE ROGERS?!*

JACQUELINE?

GOOD HEAVENS, IT *IS* YOU! YOU'VE COME BACK TO US AT LAST!

JACKIE, YOU LITTLE SPITFIRE! IT'S BEEN A LONG TIME!

TOO LONG! HERE, LET ME LOOK AT YOU!

OH, IT'S LIKE A MIRACLE. YOU HAVEN'T AGED A DAY SINCE THE WAR.

JUST THE RESULT OF AN UNPLANNED ACCIDENT, MILADY. I SPENT A FEW DECADES ON ICE... LITERALLY,

THE SCIENCE BOYS CALLED IT *SUSPENDED ANIMATION.*

YES, I KNOW... I READ ALL ABOUT IT IN THE *TIMES.*

JACKIE? IS SOMETHING WRONG?

NO, NO, IT'S JUST THAT... I'M A MESS. LET ME CLEAN UP AND THEN WE'LL TALK.

I WAS YOUNGER THAN HE WAS, AND NOW I'M OLDER... SO MUCH OLDER.

SOON, IN THE MANSION'S SOLARIUM...

ANYWAY, AFTER I CAME OFF THE ICE, MY MEMORY WAS A BIT ADDLED FOR A WHILE. THERE WERE BLANK SPACES IN MY PAST WHICH I COULDN'T ACCOUNT FOR.

WHY, IN MY FIRST OUTING WITH THE AVENGERS, I DIDN'T EVEN RECOGNIZE THE SUB-MARINER!* IT WAS JUST RECENTLY THAT MY FULL MEMORY RETURNED.**

THAT'S WHY I NEVER WROTE OR CALLED.

NO NEED TO APOLOGIZE, STEVE. I QUITE UNDERSTAND.

*AVENGERS #4
**CAP #247 --
JIM.

THINGS HERE HAVE, OF COURSE, CHANGED OVER THE YEARS.

MY POWERS AS SPITFIRE GRADUALLY FADED WITH TIME, AND MY BROTHER BRIAN-- THE SECOND UNION JACK-- DIED IN AN AUTO ACCIDENT IN 1953.

I MARRIED LORD CRICHTON IN '56... I WAS WIDOWED JUST THREE YEARS AGO.

I'M... SORRY, I...

MY PERIOD OF MOURNING HAS PASSED, STEVE. BE-SIDES, I DO HAVE A FINE YOUNG SON, KENNETH, WHO'S AWAY AT SCHOOL. I MOVED BACK HERE A YEAR AGO TO LOOK AFTER FATHER.

OH, BUT YOU HAVEN'T TOLD ME WHAT BRINGS YOU HERE!

WHY... I CAME IN ANSWER TO YOUR CABLE FOR HELP!

CABLE? I SENT NO CABLE!

NO. I SENT THE CABLE!

LORD FALSWORTH!

I KNEW YOU'D COME, STEVEN! I ALWAYS COULD COUNT ON YOU!

GOOD TO SEE YOU, SIR! I HADN'T EXPECTED... THAT IS...

SURPRISED TO SEE ME AMONG THE LIVING? HAH! WE FALSWORTHS ARE A HEARTY BREED!

BUT THERE IS BUSINESS AT HAND--DEADLY BUSINESS! THERE'VE BEEN A SERIES OF MURDERS IN THIS AREA RECENTLY. THE POLICE ARE CALLING THE MURDERER THE SLASHER... BUT I BELIEVE THAT HE'S OUR OLD WARTIME FOE... BARON BLOOD!

FATHER, THAT'S RIDICULOUS! BARON BLOOD IS DEAD!

NO, HE IS UNDEAD, JACQUELINE... A VAM-PIRE, AS WELL YOU SHOULD RECALL! AND EACH OF THE SO-CALLED SLASHER'S VICTIMS HAVE BEEN DRAINED OF THEIR BLOOD!

I TOLD YOU BEFORE, THE CONSTABLE THINKS THE SLASHER IS SOME LUNATIC-- ONE WHO PERHAPS THINKS HE'S A VAMPIRE!

POPPYCOCK! BLOOD IS A MASTER OF TRICKERY! HE'S FOOLED THEM SOMEHOW, I CAN FEEL IT IN MY BONES!

AT ANY RATE, HE'S NOT BARON BLOOD! I HAD SCOTLAND YARD CHECK, AND BLOOD'S REMAINS ARE STILL ENTOMBED IN THE TOWER OF LONDON, WHERE THEY'VE BEEN SINCE THE WAR!

I TRIED TO CONVINCE THE CROWN TO PERMANENTLY PUT AN END TO BARON BLOOD YEARS AGO-- BUT, NO, THEY WOULDN'T LISTEN!

[137]

THERE'S ONLY ONE WAY TO TOTALLY DESTROY A VAMPIRE ... DECAPITATION! AND THEN THE HEAD AND BODY MUST BE BURNT SEPARATELY!

I UNDERSTAND, SIR. I'LL CHECK THINGS OUT FOR YOU!

PLEASE, SIR... IT'S TIME FOR YOUR MEDICINE!

OH, VERY WELL, HOTCHKINS! STEVEN, I'M AN OLD MAN, BUT YOU--!

BLESS, YOU, SON!

I'M SORRY, STEVE. I'M AFRAID THAT FATHER HAS BECOME A BIT SENILE.

DON'T SAY THAT, JACKIE-- DON'T EVER SAY THAT! HE MAY BE OLD AND ENFEEBLED--

--BUT I SAW THE LOOK IN THOSE EYES. HIS MIND IS STILL AS SHARP AND CLEAR AS THE DAYS WHEN HE WAS UNION JACK!

AND IF HE THINKS BARON BLOOD IS BEHIND THESE MURDERS, THEN CAPTAIN AMERICA IS GOING TO INVESTIGATE! I OWE HIM THAT MUCH!

A SHORT TIME LATER, IN THE OFFICES OF THE VILLAGE DOCTOR...

YOU'LL BE FINE, JENNY. JUST KEEP TAKING THAT IRON SUPPLEMENT, AND YOU'LL BE BRIGHT AND FULL OF ENERGY IN NO TIME!

Y-YES, DOCTOR.

BEGGIN' YOUR PARDON, DOCTOR CROMWELL, BUT THERE'S A GENTLEMAN HERE WHO'D LIKE TO ASK YOU A FEW QUESTIONS!

CAPTAIN AMERICA! I SAY, THIS IS AN HONOR, SIR! I SAW YOU IN ACTION DURING THE WAR, I DID!

I'M SORRY I CAN'T SAY I RECOGNIZE YOU, DOCTOR... BUT I HAD A FEELING WE'D MET BEFORE.

I UNDERSTAND THAT YOU'VE INSPECTED THE BODIES OF THE SLASHER'S VICTIMS!

YES, I DOUBLE AS THE LOCAL CORONER. THIS SLASHER BUSINESS IS A DIRTY ONE... MURDER AND MUTILATION... OBVIOUSLY THE WORK OF A SICK MIND.

OBVIOUSLY, BUT, ISN'T THERE A POSSIBILITY THAT IT COULD ALSO BE THE WORK OF A VAMPIRE?

WHAT?!

HOW... HOW DARE YOU MENTION SUCH SUPERSTITIOUS CLAP-TRAP IN MY PRESENCE?!

GET OUT!, OUT OF MY OFFICES! I DON'T CARE WHO YOU ARE-- I'LL NOT HAVE SUCH LUNACY PROPOUNDED HERE!

BUT, I...

OUT!!

[138]

SORRY ABOUT THAT, CAPTAIN. I SHOULD'VE WARNED YOU THAT THE DOCTOR IS SENSITIVE ON THE SUBJECT OF VAMPIRES.

YOU PROBABLY NOTICED THEM SCARS ON 'IS FACE. WELL, HE GOT 'EM A FEW YEARS BACK, WHEN HE WAS BRAND NEW TO THE VILLAGE.

THERE WAS A VAMPIRE SCARE IN THESE PARTS BACK THEN. SOME CLAIMED THAT DRACULA 'IMSELF WAS IN THE LAND.

WELL, SIR, SOME OF THE LOCALS THOUGHT THEY'D TRAPPED A VAMPIRE IN THE DOCTOR'S COTTAGE, SO THEY TORCHED THE PLACE!

"DOC CROMWELL ARRIVED TO SEE HIS HOUSE GO UP IN FLAMES. THE TOWNSFOLK HADN'T KNOWN HIS DAUGHTER WAS INSIDE.

"HE RUSHED IN TO SAVE HER... BUT IT WAS TOO LATE FOR THE GIRL. HE WAS PRETTY BADLY BURNED AS WELL. HE GREW THAT BEARD TO COVER THE WORST OF THE SCARS."

I CAN UNDERSTAND THE DOCTOR'S REACTION. BUT VAMPIRES *DO* EXIST-- MY BATTLES WITH BARON BLOOD DURING THE WAR PROVED THAT TO ME... ALL TOO WELL.

IF DOCTOR CROMWELL WON'T HELP ME, I'LL JUST HAVE TO LOOK ELSEWHERE.

IN ONE FORM OR ANOTHER, THE CASTLE-LIKE STRUCTURE KNOWN AS THE TOWER OF LONDON HAS STOOD HERE ON THE BANKS OF THE THAMES FOR SOME 900 YEARS!

MUCH HISTORY IS TIED UP IN THE DARK PASSAGEWAYS OF THE TOWER... AND IT IS RUMORED THAT THE GHOST OF ANNE BOLEYN-- SECOND WIFE OF KING HENRY VIII -- OFTEN WALKS THE TOWER HALLS.

BUT IT'S NO GHOST WHO ROAMS THESE CORRIDORS THIS AFTERNOON. NO, THIS IS A *LIVING* LEGEND.

I APPRECIATE SCOTLAND YARD BEING SO COOPERATIVE, INSPECTOR SWEENEY,

YOU WERE SAYING THAT BARON BLOOD'S BODY HAS LAIN IN STATE HERE ALL THESE YEARS?

THAT'S CORRECT, SIR. HE WAS LORD FALSWORTH'S BROTHER, AFTER ALL, AND THE LEGAL QUESTION OF HOW TO DISPOSE OF A MEMBER OF NOBILITY--

--EVEN IF HE WAS... WELL... UNDEAD --WAS NEVER SATISFACTORILY DECIDED.

STILL AND ALL, WE'VE TAKEN EVERY POSSIBLE PRECAUTION. BLOOD'S TOMB HERE IS FESTOONED WITH GARLIC... RELIGIOUS ICONS... ALL THINGS ABHORRENT TO VAMPIRES!

UNLOCK THE VAULT, REG!

YES SIR, INSPECTOR.

THERE, CAPTAIN... BLOOD'S BIER... SEALED AND UNTOUCHED ALL THESE DECADES.

SO IT APPEARS. BUT THERE'S ONLY ONE WAY TO BE SURE.

RIGHT YOU ARE.

WITH CAREFUL, DELIBERATE MOVEMENTS, INSPECTOR SWEENEY LOOSENS A SERIES OF CLAMPS THAT HOLD ON THE HEAVY IRON LID. AND THEN...

THERE HE IS, CAPTAIN. NOT A PRETTY SIGHT, I'LL GRANT YOU-- BUT AS YOU CAN SEE, THERE'S NO WAY BARON BLOOD COULD BE THE SLASHER!

YOU'RE WRONG, INSPECTOR --DEAD WRONG!

GOOD LORD, MAN, HAVE YOU TAKEN LEAVE OF YOUR SENSES? PUT THAT STAKE BACK OR THE VAMPIRE WILL REVIVE!

EH?

WE'VE NOTHING TO FEAR FROM *THIS* BODY, INSPECTOR!

THIS ISN'T A VAMPIRE! THIS ISN'T EVEN THE SKELETON OF A MAN!

SOON, IN THE CORONER'S LAB AT NEW SCOTLAND YARD...

'E'S RIGHT, INSPECTOR. THAT'S THE BODY OF A TWENTY-YEAR-OLD WOMAN... BEEN DEAD ABOUT TWELVE YEARS, I'D SAY. NO TELLIN' HOW LONG SHE'S BEEN IN THE TOWER!

INCREDIBLE!

I KNEW THAT BODY DIDN'T LOOK RIGHT! I'VE SEEN MANY-- TOO MANY --IN COMBAT.

BUT THIS MEANS THAT BARON BLOOD MAY HAVE BEEN LOOSE FOR A DECADE OR MORE! IT DOESN'T MEAN THAT HE'S THE SLASHER... BUT HE'S A VERY GOOD SUSPECT!

YEAH. LOOKS LIKE I OWE YOU AND LORD FALSWORTH AN APOLOGY, CAP. I DON'T KNOW HOW THIS COULD'VE HAPPENED, BUT I PROMISE YOU WE'LL LAUNCH AN IMMEDIATE INVESTIGATION.

GOOD. YOU CAN COUNT ON ME FOR ASSISTANCE, INSPECTOR. IF YOU NEED ME, I'LL BE STAYING AT FALSWORTH MANOR.

AND SO, AS NIGHT FALLS...

IF BARON BLOOD *IS* THIS SLASHER CHARACTER, THEN I'M SURE HE'LL STRIKE BEFORE TOO LONG.

OF COURSE, BLOOD COULD HAVE LEFT FOR SOME REMOTE CORNER OF THE WORLD... BUT I DOUBT THAT VERY MUCH. HE'S TOO TIED TO THIS AREA!

ENTERING THE MANSION, CAP FINDS JACQUELINE FALSWORTH-CRICHTON IN THE MIDST OF A FAMILY DISAGREEMENT.

IF YOU WERE GOING TO BRING YOUR... YOUR FRIEND HOME FOR THE HOLIDAYS, YOU MIGHT HAVE AT LEAST GIVEN ME SOME WARNING.

UH... PARDON ME. I HOPE I'M NOT INTERRUPTING ANYTHING.

DON'T HAND ME THAT, MOTHER-- IT'S NOT THE LACK OF WARNING THAT ANNOYS YOU! YOU JUST DON'T LIKE ME PALLING AROUND WITH JOEY! YOU THINK HE'S TOO LOW CLASS!

WELL, IF YOU WISH ME TO BE BLUNT--!

WE'LL DISCUSS THIS LATER, KENNETH. YOUR ART SCHOOL CHUM CAN STAY... FOR THE TIME BEING.

DO COME IN, CAP! I WANT YOU TO MEET MY SON-- KENNETH CRICHTON.

MY PLEASURE, SIR. MUM'S ALWAYS SPOKEN VERY HIGHLY OF YOU.

KEN...

YUH, AN' I'M JOEY CHAPMAN! KEN AN' ME ARE BEST MATES AT THE ART SCHOOL, Y'KNOW.

COR, I NEVER THOUGHT I'D BE SHAKIN' HANDS WITH CAP'N AMERICA. ME UNCLE USTA TELL ME YARNS 'BOUT YOU! YOU'RE IN RIGHT GOOD SHAPE FOR AN OLD SOD!

PLEASED TO MEET YOU, JOEY. YOU SEEM TO BE IN FAIRLY GOOD SHAPE YOURSELF. THAT'S... SOME GRIP YOU HAVE!

YUH, KEN AN' ME ARE BOTH ON A WRESTLIN' TEAM. CARE TO GO A FEW ROUNDS?

I HOPE YOU BOYS CAN DELAY YOUR MATCH UNTIL I HAVE A CHANCE TO SPEAK WITH THE CAPTAIN.

WELL, CAP... WHAT DID YOU LEARN?

NOTHING FOR CERTAIN ABOUT THE IDENTITY OF THE SLASHER, LORD FALSWORTH... BUT YOU *WERE* RIGHT--

--BARON BLOOD IS ON THE LOOSE!

I KNEW IT! *I KNEW IT!* HE *HAS* TO BE THE SLASHER! NO ONE WILL BE SAFE FROM MY ACCURSED DEMON-BROTHER UNTIL HE IS FINALLY ELIMINATED FOR ALL TIME!

FATHER, PLEASE! REMEMBER YOUR HEART!

CAP, ARE YOU CERTAIN--?

[141]

VERY CERTAIN, JACKIE. NOW, IF YOU'LL EXCUSE US, I THINK I SHOULD CONFER WITH HIS LORDSHIP FOR A WHILE ... IN PRIVATE.

NOT MEANIN' TO BE DISRESPECTFUL, KENNY--BUT IS YOUR GRANDPOP ALL THERE? HE DON'T SOUND LIKE IT!

I DON'T KNOW, JOEY. BUT IT HURTS TO SEE HIM LIKE THIS.

SHORTLY, IN THE LIBRARY...

STEVEN, BARON BLOOD ROBBED ME OF THE USE OF MY LEGS-- AND TIME HAS SAPPED MY STRENGTH AND MY HEALTH. SOMETIMES I FEEL LIKE MY MIND IS ALL THAT'S LEFT ME.

TELL ME... HONESTLY... AM I LOSING THAT, TOO?

THEY ALL THINK I'M MAD.

I KNOW, SIR.

NO, LORD FALSWORTH--YOU'RE AS SANE AS ANY MAN. WE CAN'T BE SURE THAT BARON BLOOD IS THE SLASHER, BUT I AGREE THAT HE PROBABLY IS. THESE VILLAGE MURDERS MAY BE SOME SORT OF MAD WARNING.

WHATEVER THE CASE, I'M WILLING TO STAY HERE UNTIL WE GET TO THE BOTTOM OF THIS, AND I PROMISE YOU--

--WE *WILL* FIND BARON BLOOD. AND WE WILL *STOP* HIM.

WHEN I HEAR YOU TALK LIKE THAT, CAP, IT TAKES ME BACK TO THE WAR.

THOSE WERE HORRIBLE DAYS, TO BE SURE... DARK DAYS. BUT SOMEHOW, THE WORLD SEEMED MORE INNOCENT THEN... MORE HOPEFUL.

THANK YOU FOR COMING IN ANSWER TO MY CABLE, STEVE... THANK YOU.

BY THE TIME THE MOON IS FULL IN THE SKIES, FALSWORTH MANOR HAS GROWN DARK,...

...A GREAT STONY FORTRESS AMID THE ROLLING BRITISH COUNTRYSIDE.

BUT ALONG ONE CORNICE OF THE STRUCTURE SKULKS A TWISTED, GARGOYLE-LIKE FORM....

...A FIGURE NOT OF STONE AND MORTAR, BUT OF UNLIVING FLESH AND BONE!

THIS IS *BARON BLOOD!*

THE MANOR HAS GROWN SILENT! NOW SHALL I STRIKE!

CREEPING OVER THE STONEWORK OF THE MANSE, THE VAMPIRE SKITTERS DOWN THE SIDE OF THE BUILDING, HEAD FIRST-- LIKE SOME HUGE, HIDEOUS SPIDER--

--UNTIL HE COMES TO AN OPENED WINDOW!

THEN, HE PAUSES, AN AWFUL, BARELY AUDIBLE LAUGH RASPING DEEP IN HIS THROAT.

JUST AS I THOUGHT! CAPTAIN AMERICA HAS BEEN GIVEN THE SAME GUEST ROOM HE USED DURING WORLD WAR TWO!

THE FALSWORTHS AND THEIR PENCHANT FOR SENTIMENTALITY HAVE DOOMED THE YANKEE!

SLOWLY--

--THE GROTESQUE FIGURE SLIDES INTO THE ROOM, INCHING EVER CLOSER TO HIS INTENDED TARGET...

ONE SWIFT SNAP OF THE NECK, AND CAPTAIN AMERICA WILL NO LONGER BE A PROBLEM FOR ANYONE!

I'M NOT GOING TO BE THAT EASY A VICTIM, BLOOD!

≶WHUUUNGH!≶

YOUR HATRED FOR YOUR FORMER FAMILY ALWAYS WAS YOUR WEAK SPOT, BLOOD! ONCE I LEARNED THAT YOU WERE FREE--

--I KNEW THAT YOU'D HAVE TO COME BACK HERE SOONER OR LATER, AND I HOPED THAT YOU'D FIND ME MORE OF A CHALLENGING TARGET THAN YOUR AGED BROTHER OR JACKIE.

LOOKS LIKE I WAS RIGHT.

BARON BLOOD'S ONLY ANSWER IS A LOW, FERAL SNARL AND A SWIFT SUDDEN--

--DEVASTATING BLOW!

KERESH

I WAS CARELESS! I HAVE TO KEEP REMINDING MYSELF THAT BLOOD'S STRENGTH IS SUPERNATURAL IN NATURE-- THAT HE'S SO MUCH STRONGER THAN HE LOOKS!

YOU HAVE SEALED YOUR FATE, CAPTAIN! I HAD PLANNED TO MERELY END YOUR MISERABLE LIFE ... BUT NOW, YOU SHALL JOIN ME IN UNDEATH!

I DOUBT THAT.

I'VE PREPARED FOR YOU, BARON! THIS LOOP OF GARLIC SHOULD BE ENOUGH TO SLOW DOWN THE MIGHTIEST VAMPIRE!

AARRGH!

CURSE YOU! CURSE THIS DRATTED HERB-- ITS TOUCH IS AS REPUGNANT TO ME AS ITS SCENT!

YOU'VE GOT A LOT OF GALL, TALKING ABOUT REPUGNANCE, BLOOD! WHAT ABOUT THOSE SLASHER MURDERS... THOSE THREE INNO-CENT WOMEN? DON'T YOU HAVE ANY CONSCIENCE AT ALL?

CONSCIENCE IS FOR LESSER BEINGS!

EH? HE'S GONE ... TURNED INTO MIST!

OF COURSE, FOOL! IS THAT NOT WITHIN THE POWER OF THE UNDEAD?!

KRAK

I DON'T CARE WHAT YOU TURN YOURSELF INTO, BLOOD-- I'LL STILL FIND A WAY TO STOP YOU!

YOU'RE A BOLD MAN, CAPTAIN-- BUT YOU ARE ONLY A MAN... WHEREAS I AM A SCION OF DRACULA, THE LORD OF VAM-PIRES! MINE IS THE POWER--

[145]

"-- TO CONTROL THE FOG, THE WOLF, AND THE VERMIN OF THE EARTH! EVEN NOW, MY ARMY OF THE NIGHT IS SURROUNDING FALSWORTH MANOR!"

"THE LONGER WE BATTLE, THE CLOSER THEY CREEP TOWARDS MY DEAR, DAMNED BROTHER AND HIS FAMILY!"

INDEED, AT THAT MOMENT, IN ANOTHER WING OF THE MANOR...

MOTHER! WHAT ON EARTH IS THAT BLOODY RACKET?

I... I DON'T KNOW, BUT IT SEEMS TO BE COMING FROM THE DIRECTION OF YOUR GRANDFATHER'S ROOM!

BUT BETWEEN JACQUELINE AND THE AWFUL NOISE, A MORE SILENT STRUGGLE RAGES BETWEEN TWO OLD FOES...

YOU CANNOT LONG RESIST THE FULL STRENGTH OF THE VAMPIRE!

HE'S RIGHT. YET, FOR ALL OF BLOOD'S POWER, HE CAN STILL BE TAKEN BY SURPRISE!

AND WITH MY KNOWLEDGE OF LEVERAGE, I CAN USE HIS STRENGTH AGAINST HIM!

WITH A SPLIT-SECOND TIMING THAT DEFIES BELIEF, CAP SUDDENLY SHIFTS HIS WEIGHT, PROPELLING BARON BLOOD OVER HIM AND INTO THE NEXT ROOM!

WHAT? BARON BLOOD... HERE?

LEAPING TO HIS FEET, BARON BLOOD IGNORES THE FEEBLE GASP OF HIS MORTAL BROTHER, TURNING INSTEAD TOWARDS CAPTAIN AMERICA... HIS EYES ABLAZE IN THE SEMI-DARKNESS!

I TIRE OF THIS BATTLE, CAPTAIN!

THERE IS NO NEED FOR ME TO WASTE MY TIME IN USELESS COMBAT, WHEN MY HYPNOTIC POWERS CAN HALT YOU IN YOUR TRACKS!

1940! As the world teetered on the brink of global war, frail **Steve Rogers** entered a secret laboratory and was transformed into the American **super-soldier!** For four thrilling years, he battled the Axis powers — until a freak stroke of fate threw him into **suspended animation.** When he awoke, he was a man decades out of his time! Since that fateful day, Steve Rogers has sought his destiny in this brave new world!

STAN LEE PRESENTS: CAPTAIN AMERICA!

BLOOD ON THE MOORS

CAPTAIN AMERICA STANDS STOCK STILL, ENTRANCED BY THE IRRESISTIBLE MESMERIZING POWER OF BARON BLOOD--

--WHO CRAWLS OVER HIS VICTIM, READY TO SINK FANGS INTO THE HERO-- AND TURN THE LIVING LEGEND INTO AN UNDEAD MONSTER!

AT THE DOOR OF THE CHAMBER, LADY JACQUELINE FALSWORTH-CRICHTON AND HER SON, KENNETH, STAND TRANSFIXED BY THE HORRIFYING TABLEAU...

...WHILE OLD, ENFEEBLED LORD FALSWORTH-- WHO WAS ONCE THE BRITISH HERO KNOWN AS UNION JACK-- STRUGGLES TO SIT UP IN HIS BED, UNABLE TO SAVE HIS OLD FRIEND!

ROGER STERN & JOHN BYRNE
WRITER / CO-PLOTTERS / PENCILER
JOSEF RUBINSTEIN
INKER
JOE ROSEN, LETTERER
BOB SHAREN, COLORIST
JIM SALICRUP, EDITOR
JIM SHOOTER, PEER
SPECIAL THANKS TO COLIN CAMPBELL FOR HIS KIND ASSISTANCE!

[149]

BARON BLOOD EAGERLY CLOSES IN ON CAP'S THROAT, HIS FETID BREATH ASSAULTING THE HERO'S NOSTRILS AS CAP DESPERATELY TRIES TO BREAK FREE OF THE VAMPIRE'S CONTROL.

A MILLION QUESTIONS RACE THROUGH THE AVENGER'S MIND... HOW DID HE COME TO THIS PREDICAMENT? WHAT IS HE DOING HERE, IN ENGLAND?

AS IF WADING THROUGH A THICK FOG, THE ANSWERS COME TO MIND...

IT HAD ALL BEGUN A MERE 24 HOURS AGO, WITH THE DISCOVERY OF A MURDER VICTIM'... A YOUNG WOMAN, DRAINED OF BLOOD. SHE HAD NOT BEEN THE FIRST TO DIE IN SUCH A MANNER.

LEARNING OF THE MURDER, LORD FALSWORTH SENT A SPECIAL CODED MESSAGE-- REQUESTING ASSISTANCE-- TO CAPTAIN AMERICA, IN CARE OF AVENGERS MANSION.

AND THOUGH THE MESSAGE WAS RELAYED BY PHONE TO CAP'S ALTER EGO, STEVE ROGERS, AT AN INOPPORTUNE MOMENT--

--CAP IMMEDIATELY LEFT FOR ENGLAND. THERE HE FOUND THAT THE OLD LORD BELIEVED THE MURDERER TO BE THEIR WARTIME FOE, BARON BLOOD.

FALSWORTH'S FAMILY HOWEVER, THOUGHT THE OLD MAN TO BE SENILE. NO ONE BELIEVED HIM... LEAST OF ALL KEN'S SCHOOL CHUM, JOEY CHAPMAN!

BUT, AS NIGHT FELL, BARON BLOOD DID INDEED STRIKE... AT FALSWORTH MANOR ITSELF!

STEALTHILY, THE VAMPIRE ENTERED CAP'S ROOM AND PREPARED TO END THE AVENGER'S LIFE WITH A QUICK TWIST OF THE NECK.

BUT CAP WAS PREPARED FOR SUCH AN ATTACK, AND IMMEDIATELY LAUNCHED AN ALL-OUT OFFENSIVE AGAINST THE VAMPIRE...

...UNTIL THE BARON MANAGED TO ENTHRALL HIS ENEMY.

AND NOW, THE VAMPIRE'S FANGS ARE BUT INCHES AWAY FROM CAPTAIN AMERICA'S JUGULAR VEIN!

NOTHING CAN SAVE HIM NOW!

EH?

KRUNK

NOTHING, THAT IS, EXCEPT THE THIN LAYER OF CHAIN MAIL WHICH COVERS HIS NECK!

PAIN... CLEARING MY HEAD! THANK HEAVEN FOR SMALL FAVORS!

≋MMUMPH!≋

BLAST YOU AND YOUR ACCURSED PROTECTIVE UNIFORM! IF I CAN'T BITE YOUR NECK, AT LEAST I CAN STILL BREAK IT!

THREATS ARE ONE THING, BARON-- RESULTS ARE SOMETHING ELSE!

CAP, WATCH OUT!

NO NEED TO WORRY, KEN! IT DOESN'T MATTER HOW STRONG, HOW POWERFUL AN OPPONENT IS...

...EVEN THE MIGHTIEST BEINGS CAN BE DEFEATED WITH THE PROPER APPLICATION OF LEVERAGE!

KRAK

YOU'LL NOT MAKE MOCK OF ME WITH YOUR ACROBATIC TRICKS, CAPTAIN! SOONER OR LATER, I'LL GET YOU!

IT'S JUST A MATTER OF TIME!

YOU CAN THINK AGAIN, YOU BLOODY MONSTER! YOU'LL NOT HARM ANYONE IN THIS HOUSEHOLD!

NO, KEN-- LET ME HANDLE BARON BLOOD! YOU HAVE NO IDEA HOW DEADLY HE CAN BE!

I CAN RESIST THE SUN'S RAYS FOR A TIME IN THIS FORM, BUT MY POWERS ARE GREATLY WEAKENED. I MUST FLEE WHILE THERE IS STILL TIME!

CAP! YOU MUST STOP HIM... HE MUSTN'T ESCAPE!

DON'T WORRY, LORD FALSWORTH, HE'S NOT GETTING AWAY THAT EASILY!

THERE ARE AT LEAST THREE MURDERS YOU HAVE TO ANSWER FOR, BARON-- NOT TO MENTION YOUR WAR CRIMES!

I'LL ANSWER FOR NOTHING, YANKEE FOOL!

GATHERING ALL HIS STRENGTH, CAP MAKES A GREAT LEAP AFTER THE FLEEING VAMPIRE...

...BUT THE CREATURE HE GRABS FOR NO LONGER POSSESSES THE SIZE OR FORM OF A MAN!

WITH A FLAPPING OF LEATHERN WINGS, THE BAT ELUDES CAP'S GRASP--

--AND THE STAR-SPANGLED AVENGER PLUMMETS FROM THE UPPER STORY WINDOW!

WITH A SKILL THAT WOULD ASTOUND A CHAMPION GYMNAST, CAP SUDDENLY TWISTS ABOUT IN MIDAIR-- SNAGGING HOLD OF AN OUTSTRETCHED TREE LIMB, SWINGING HIMSELF AROUND--

--AND LANDING SAFELY ON THE GROUND, YET, EVEN AS HE LANDS, HIS THOUGHTS ARE NOT OF HIMSELF OR HIS NARROW ESCAPE--

--BUT OF HIS FOE'S SURPRISING GETAWAY!

INCREDIBLE! BARON BLOOD HAS THE FULL POWERS OF A VAMPIRE! I'D ASSUMED THAT THE TREATMENTS THE NAZI SURGEONS GAVE HIM DURING THE WAR *-- TO HELP HIM RESIST SUNLIGHT-- HAD CANCELED OUT ANY SHAPE-CHANGING ABILITIES!

IT APPEARS THAT I WAS WRONG. WELL, THAT'S ONE MISTAKE I WON'T MAKE AGAIN.

OUR NEXT ENCOUNTER WILL BE OUR LAST, BARON... ONE WAY OR ANOTHER!

*SEE INVADERS #9 --JIM.

ALL RIGHT, JOEY, I'LL ACCEPT KEN'S WORD THAT YOU'RE ON THE UP-AND-UP. BUT WATCH YOUR STEP!

COME ON, JACKIE-- WE'RE CALLING ON SCOTLAND YARD!

@X!☆!@※!!% AMERICAN!

WAR HERO OR NOT, I'M STARTIN' TO GET JUST A LITTLE BLOODY TIRED OF THE RIGHTEOUS CAPTAIN AMERICA, KENNY.

YOU WOULDN'T BE SO DOWN ON THE MAN, IF YOU'D SEEN WHAT HE WENT THROUGH THIS MORNING, JOEY. BARON BLOOD MAY SOUND LIKE A BAD FAIRY TALE, BUT HE'S ALL TOO REAL.

"YOU SEE, JUST BEFORE THE FIRST WORLD WAR, MY GREAT GRANDFATHER DIED-- AND MOTHER'S FATHER, AS ELDEST SON, BECAME THE NEW LORD FALSWORTH.

"GRANDFATHER'S YOUNGER BROTHER INHERITED BUT A SMALL ALLOTMENT, AND A GREAT DEAL OF BITTERNESS!

AND, GOD HELP US, HE'S MY GREAT-UNCLE!

"AT ANY RATE, THE BROTHER SET OUT TO BETTER HIS FORTUNES ON THE CONTINENT, EVENTUALLY ARRIVING IN THE REMOTE SECTION OF ROMANIA KNOWN AS TRANSYLVANIA!

"THERE, IN A CRYPT DEEP BENEATH AN ANCIENT CASTLE, HE FOUND THE RESTING PLACE OF THE ONE HE SOUGHT-- THE FABLED LORD OF VAMPIRES, *DRACULA!*

"IN HIS MAD AMBITION, HE SOUGHT TO ATTAIN POWER THROUGH CONTROL OF THE VAMPIRE-LORD.

"BUT HE HAD NOT RECKONED WITH DRACULA'S INCREDIBLE HYPNOTIC POWERS!

"OVERCOME BY THE VAMPIRE'S STARE, HE DROPPED HIS PROTECTIVE CROSS, AND BECAME YET ANOTHER UNDEAD MINION OF DRACULA!

"AT HIS COMMAND, MY GREAT-UNCLE RETURNED TO ENGLAND, TO WREAK HAVOC ON THE HOMELAND OF DRACULA'S LONGTIME ENEMIES, THE HARKER FAMILY.

"AND, AS THE WAR BROKE OUT, HE BECAME A DEADLY AGENT IN THE SERVICE OF THE GERMAN KAISER...

"...HE BECAME *BARON BLOOD!*

"BETWEEN THE WORLD WARS, THE BARON DROPPED OUT OF SIGHT, EVENTUALLY ALLYING HIMSELF WITH A CAUSE AS EVIL AS VAMPIRISM...

"...HITLER'S THIRD REICH!

[155]

"RETURNING TO ENGLAND DURING WORLD WAR TWO, BARON BLOOD CAME BACK TO FALSWORTH MANOR IN THE GUISE OF ONE JOHN FALSWORTH, THE *SON* OF GRAND-FATHER'S 'DEAR DEPARTED BROTHER.'"

HELLO, CAPTAIN... JACQUELINE! BEAUTIFUL MORNING, WOT?

"SHORTLY THEREAFTER, MOTHER NEARLY SUC-CUMBED TO THE BARON'S BITE. INDEED, SHE WOULD PROBABLY HAVE BECOME AN 'UNDEAD' HERSELF, WERE IT NOT FOR THE TIMELY INTER-VENTION OF THAT WARTIME SUPER-TEAM, *THE INVADERS!*"

"BARON BLOOD WAS DEFEATED IN THAT BATTLE, BUT AT A TERRIBLE PRICE! GRANDFATHER'S LEGS WERE CRUSHED, LEAVING HIM A CRIPPLE FOR LIFE..."

"...AND MOTHER'S LIFE WAS SAVED ONLY BY AN EMERGENCY TRANS-FUSION OF BLOOD--

"--FROM THE ANDROID KNOWN AS THE *HUMAN TORCH!*

"STILL AND ALL, OUT OF THAT TRAGIC BATTLE WAS BORN A NEW SUPER-BEING. FOR THE STRANGE ARTIFICIAL BLOOD OF THE TORCH TRANSFORMED MOTHER INTO THE SUPER-FAST *SPITFIRE!*

MOTHER'S SPEED FADED WITH THE PASSAGE OF TIME, OF COURSE. AND MY UNCLE BRIAN SUCCEEDED GRANDFATHER AS THE SECOND UNION JACK.

IN FACT, BRIAN WAS STILL SEMI-ACTIVE AS UNION JACK UP UNTIL HIS DEATH IN 1953.

I THINK GRANDFATHER WOULD HAVE LIKED FOR ME TO HAVE BECOME A THIRD UNION JACK, BUT MY HEART ISN'T INTO THAT SORT OF THING. I JUST DON'T SEE MYSELF AS THE CONQUERING HERO-TYPE.

LORD, KENNY... I KNEW YOUR FAMILY HAD DONE A LOT DURING THE WAR, BUT I NEVER DREAMT THAT THEY WERE CONNECTED WITH THE INVADERS!

I GUESS... THE CAP'N WAS RIGHT TO READ ME OUT LIKE HE DID... ALL THINGS CONSIDERED.

MEANWHILE, A FEW MILES AWAY, ON THE OUTSKIRTS OF THE NEARBY VILLAGE, A DARK FORM HURRIEDLY APPROACHES AN OPEN COTTAGE WINDOW--

--AND PASSES THROUGH, ASSUMING ONCE MORE THE FORM OF A MAN.

BLAST! I'D HOPED THAT THE PASSAGE OF TIME HAD DULLED THE YANK'S BATTLE SAVVY...

...BUT, IF ANYTHING HE'S BECOME MORE FORMIDABLE THAN EVER! I SHALL HAVE TO RETHINK MY PLANS FOR REVENGE.

THAT SHALL HAVE TO WAIT, HOWEVER! FOR NOW, IT IS IMPORTANT THAT I RESUME MY PROTECTIVE DISGUISE, TO BETTER RESIST THE POWER OF THE SUN!

WITH PRACTICED MOVEMENTS, THE UNDEAD CREATURE SLIPS ON THE SPECIALLY CONSTRUCTED LIFE-MASK AND THE PADDED UNDERGARMENTS...

...AND GRADUALLY HE ASSUMES A MORE BENEVOLENT MIEN...

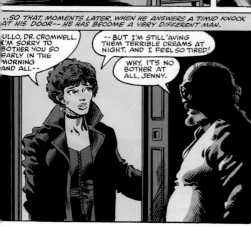

...SO THAT, MOMENTS LATER, WHEN HE ANSWERS A TIMID KNOCK AT HIS DOOR-- HE HAS BECOME A VERY DIFFERENT MAN.

'ULLO, DR. CROMWELL. I'M SORRY TO BOTHER YOU SO EARLY IN THE MORNING AND ALL--

-- BUT I'M STILL 'AVING THEM TERRIBLE DREAMS AT NIGHT, AND I FEEL SO TIRED!

WHY, IT'S NO BOTHER AT ALL, JENNY.

AFTER ALL, IT'S THE LOT OF A DOCTOR TO HELP THE TROUBLED! COME RIGHT IN...

...YOU'RE JUST IN TIME FOR... BREAKFAST!

HOURS LATER, THE MAIN HALL OF FALSWORTH MANNER BECOMES A BEEHIVE OF ACTIVITY, AS REPRESENTATIVES OF SCOTLAND YARD ASSEMBLE TO MAP OUT STRATEGY...

RIGHT! NOW, WE MUST ASSUME THAT THE VAMPIRE IS HOLED UP SOMEWHERE IN THIS IMMEDIATE VICINITY.

I AGREE, INSPECTOR SWEENEY. AS YOU KNOW, BARON BLOOD IS AT HIS WEAKEST BY DAY, AND SINCE HE NOW SEEMS TO HAVE FULL VAMPIRIC POWERS--

--HE MAY EVEN BE FORCED TO SPEND HIS DAYS IN A COFFIN. THAT'S JUST A THEORY, OF COURSE.

WHATEVER THE CASE, A SEARCH OF THE SURROUNDING AREA IS DEFINITELY IN ORDER. IT'S URGENT THAT WE FIND BLOOD BEFORE NIGHTFALL.

I WANT TO HELP IN THE SEARCH, CAP, I KNOW THE AREA AND... WELL, I NEVER THOUGHT I'D SAY THIS, BUT DESTROYING BARON BLOOD IS KIND OF A FAMILY DUTY!

IF KENNY WANTS IN ON THIS, THEN SO DO I... IF YOU'LL HAVE ME, CAP'N.

ALL RIGHT. WE CAN USE ALL THE MANPOWER WE CAN MUSTER FOR THIS.

THEY'VE PRACTICALLY FORGOTTEN I'M HERE. BARON BLOOD IS MY BROTHER... AND MY ENEMY, BUT TIME HAS STOLEN THIS BATTLE FROM ME!

IF ONLY I COULD STAND... IF ONLY UNION JACK COULD LIVE AGAIN!

AND SO, WHILE LORD FALSWORTH SITS HELPLESSLY BY, THE SEARCH BEGINS FOR A MAN LONG UNDEAD.

A CREW OF SPECIALLY TRAINED LAW OFFICERS SCOUR THE CAVES AT THE EDGE OF THE FALSWORTH ESTATE--

--EVEN AS CAP AND THE INSPECTOR QUESTION THE TOWNSPEOPLE OF THE NEARBY VILLAGE.

AND YOU'RE SURE YOU'VE NEITHER HEARD NOR SEEN ANYTHING UNUSUAL OF LATE?

SORRY, WE CAN'T HELP YE, MR. SWEENEY. ASIDE FROM THEM STRANGE MURDERS, EVERYTHING'S BEEN QUIET AS DEATH ITSELF!

NO STONE IS LEFT UNTURNED. EVERY CEMETERY IS CHECKED FOR SIGNS OF RECENT DISINTERMENT. EVERY VICAR IS CONSULTED AND WARNED OF THE VAMPIRE'S SUSPECTED PRESENCE.

A HOUSE-TO-HOUSE SEARCH IS INSTITUTED, BUT EVERYWHERE THE RESULTS ARE THE SAME...

...BARON BLOOD IS NOWHERE TO BE FOUND!

BY LATE AFTERNOON, TWO YOUNG VOLUNTEERS--FRUSTRATED BY THE FRUITLESS SEARCH--RETIRE TO THEIR FAVORITE PUB TO MULL THINGS OVER...

CHARABANC'S WELCOME

BULL & BUSH

'SO, YOU BOYS 'AVEN'T TURNED UP A THING? I'D THINK YOU'D BE GRATEFUL...

...I KNOW I'D BE SCARED TO DEATH, IF I WERE TO COME ACROSS A REAL VAMPIRE!

I DID COME ACROSS HIM, JENNY--JUST LAST NIGHT! HE'S A GHASTLY ENOUGH SIGHT, TO BE SURE, BUT EVEN A VAMPIRE CAN BE DEFEATED... RIGHT, JOEY?

IF YOU SAY SO, KENNY. ME, I'M STILL GETTIN' USED TO THE IDEA THAT SUCH A CREATURE COULD EXIST!

I SAY, JENNY... HAVE YOU BEEN UNWELL? YOU SEEM SO PALE AND JITTERY!

OH...IT'S JUST A TOUCH OF ANEMIA, KENNETH, DR. CROMWELL'S BEEN TREATING ME, BUT I CAN'T SEEM TO SHAKE IT!

WELL, LISTEN THEN... IF YOU AREN'T BETTER SOON, I'LL SEE ABOUT GETTING YOU IN TO SEE A SPECIALIST IN LONDON!

I CAN'T HAVE THE WOMAN I'M GOING TO MARRY BE ILL!

GO ON WITH YOU NOW, KENNETH! YOU KNOW THAT YOUR MOTHER WOULD NEVER STAND FOR YOU MARRYIN' A COMMONER! I'M JUST...

÷ OH! ÷

JENNY!

CATCH HER QUICK, KENNY!

WITHIN MOMENTS...

PUT HER ON THE COT THERE IN THE BACK ROOM, LADS. I'LL GO GET THE SMELLIN' SALTS!

PRAISE THE LORD, SHE'S COMING AROUND, BUT HER BREATHING'S SO SHALLOW! I'M TAKING THIS BLASTED CHOKER OFF OF HER!

COR', KENNY, LOOK...

...HER NECK!

[159]

AT THAT VERY MOMENT, ACROSS THE WIDE ATLANTIC, CAP RETURNS TO FALSWORTH MANOR ON THE RUN...

I WANT THE ENTIRE MANOR SURROUNDED BY AN ARMED GUARD TONIGHT! OTHERWISE, BARON BLOOD IS SURE TO GET AT THE FALSWORTHS.

I WONDER IF KEN AND JOEY HAVE TURNED UP ANYTHING? THEY HAVEN'T CHECKED IN YET.

YOUR SEARCH HAS BEEN IN VAIN, HASN'T IT, STEVE? I'M NOT SURPRISED...MY BROTHER WAS DEVIOUS, EVEN BEFORE HE DIED.

EH?

NEARLY A WHOLE DAY OF SEARCHING AND WE'VE FOUND NOTHING! I HAVE TO CALL SCOTLAND YARD FOR MORE MANPOWER!

LORD FALSWORTH... SIR... PARDON ME, BUT... WHAT THE DEVIL DO YOU THINK YOU'RE DOING?

ISN'T IT OBVIOUS?

UNION JACK HAS BEEN BARON BLOOD'S ARCH-FOE SINCE THE FIRST WORLD WAR. I INTEND TO BECOME UNION JACK ONCE AGAIN...IF ONLY FOR ONE NIGHT. I'M SURE MY BROTHER WILL BE UNABLE TO RESIST SUCH A TEMPTING TARGET.

I KNOW I STAND LITTLE CHANCE OF OVER-COMING HIM, BUT AT LEAST I'LL DRAW HIM OUT OF HIDING! I LEAVE IT TO YOU TO END MY MISERY, SHOULD HE SUCCEED IN MAKING A VAMPIRE OUT OF ME!

SIR, THIS IS TOTALLY UNNECESSARY! I ASSURE YOU THAT WE CAN PROTECT--!

PROTECT WHOM? PROTECT ME FROM MY BROTHER WHILE OTHERS NEEDLESSLY DIE? NO... I'M AN OLD MAN WHO'S OUT-LIVED HIS USEFUL-NESS.

BUT I CAN STILL BE OF SOME HELP...AS BAIT! AND NEITHER YOU NOR ANYONE ELSE SHALL DENY ME THAT ROLE!

I... I HAVEN'T HEARD THAT KIND OF POWER IN FATHER'S VOICE SINCE BRIAN DIED. I'D ALMOST FORGOTTEN THE MAN HE ONCE WAS. PERHAPS HE'S RIGHT.

NO, WHAT AM I THINKING? HE CAN NO MORE BE UNION JACK, THAN I COULD BE SPITFIRE AGAIN...TOO MANY YEARS HAVE PASSED...FOR BOTH OF US!

FATHER! HAVE YOU TAKEN TOTAL LEAVE OF YOUR SENSES? THE VERY IDEA OF YOU MASQUERADING AS UNION JACK IS... IS LUDICROUS!

DON'T INTERRUPT ME, STEVE! HE NEEDS TO HEAR THIS!

FATHER, YOU SIMPLY MUST START ACTING YOUR AGE! THE WAR IS OVER...LONG OVER!

NOW, JACKIE, I....

BUT HERE YOU ARE, STILL TRYING TO FIGHT IT! FOR YOU TO FACE BARON BLOOD WOULD BE SUICIDAL--AND I WON'T STAND FOR IT!

NOW YOU LISTEN TO ME, JACQUELINE! THAT BLOODY VAMPIRE IS A FALSWORTH--AND THE FALSWORTHS HAVE ALWAYS TAKEN RESPONSIBILITY FOR THEIR BLACK SHEEP EVEN KENNETH UNDERSTANDS THAT!

I'LL SEE BARON BLOOD VANQUISHED IF IT'S THE...LAST...

...THING... I DO.

LORD FALSWORTH!

FATHER!

ΞUNNGGHH!Ξ

MY... H-HEART!

ONCE AGAIN, THE MANOR COMES ALIVE WITH FRANTIC ACTIVITY! AND, WHEN THE FAMILY DOCTOR IS FINALLY SUMMONED TO THE AGED HERO'S BEDCHAMBERS...

I'M SORRY ABOUT THE MASK, DR. CROMWELL... BUT HIS LORDSHIP INSISTED...

GIVEN THE EVENTS OF THE PAST FEW DAYS, THAT'S QUITE UNDERSTANDABLE. AT LEAST THE CLOTH IS POROUS ENOUGH THAT IT SHOULDN'T INTERFERE WITH HIS BREATHING.

I'M GLAD YOU AT LEAST GAVE HIM HIS MEDICATION. HE SEEMS TO BE RESTING WELL ENOUGH.

UUNGH.

I THINK HE'S WAKING NOW. WHY DON'T YOU AND LADY CRICHTON WAIT OUTSIDE. THIS EXAMINATION COULD TAKE AWHILE.

OF COURSE, DOCTOR. COME ON JACKIE.

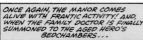

SLAM

AND NOW THAT WE HAVE SOME PRIVACY, LET US GET ON WITH OUR *'EXAMINATION'--* DEAR BROTHER!

KLIK

YES, YOU WAKING FOOL--YOUR DEVOTED DOCTOR OF THESE PAST FEW YEARS HAS BEEN *BARON BLOOD!*

OH, HOW I'VE LONGED FOR THIS MOMENT, WHEN YOU WOULD BE TOTALLY AT MY MERCY! I'VE BEEN TEMPTED SO MANY TIMES IN THE PAST MONTHS...

...BUT THE WAITING--THE PROLONGING OF YOUR WRETCHED, PITIFUL LIFE-- HAS BEEN WORTH IT!

BUT...YOU WERE DEFEATED... YOUR REMAINS LOCKED AWAY IN THE TOWER OF LONDON... HOW--?

HOW WAS I RESURRECTED? THAT WAS A BIT OF LUCK! IN RECENT YEARS, DRACULA WAS AGAIN IN THIS LAND, BROTHER! ONE OF HIS MORTAL PAWNS LEARNED OF MY EXISTENCE, AND PULLED THE STAKE FROM MY HEART, RESTORING ME!

THAT PAWN WAS THE REAL DR. CROMWELL. HE SOON BECAME MY PAWN AS WELL...I USED HIM TO GAIN CERTAIN INFORMA- TION AND KNOWLEDGE, AND WHEN HIS USEFUL- NESS WAS OVER--

--I ENDED HIS LIFE, AND THAT OF HIS DAUGHTER, TAKING HIS PLACE AS THE KINDLY COUNTRY DOCTOR!

AS DR. CROMWELL, IT WAS SIMPLE TO SUSTAIN MYSELF WITH A FEW *'ANEMIC'* PATIENTS... THOUGH I MUST ADMIT TO WEAKENING TO MY BASER COMPULSIONS OF LATE--

--AND COMMITTING THE SO-CALLED SLASHER MURDERS, BUT I WAS CAREFUL TO KILL MY VICTIMS BEFORE DRAINING THEIR BLOOD! I SHALL NOT BE SO CAREFUL WITH YOU, DEAR BROTHER...

I SHALL SLOWLY DRAIN YOUR BLOOD, AND YOU SHALL JOIN THE RANKS OF THE UNDEAD... REMAINING OLD AND FEEBLE THROUGHOUT ETERNITY!

YARRGHH!

I DON'T THINK SO, CHUM! NOT SO LONG AS THIS DIRK OF GOOD BRITISH STERLING SILVER IS BY MY SIDE!

[163]

I NEED NOT EVEN ASSUME THE FORM OF A BAT TO GET AWAY FROM YOUR INSIPID TRAP! BUT KNOW YOU THIS...

...BARON BLOOD SHALL RETURN! AND WHEN I DO, THERE SHALL BE NO MERCY SHOWN... *NONE!* ALL SHALL DIE FROM MY VAMPIRIC BITE!

YES, WHEN I RETURN, FALSWORTH MANOR WILL ECHO WITH THE CRIES OF THE NEWLY UNDEAD!

BUT, FASTER *BY* FAR THAN THE GLIDING BARON BLOOD IS THE WHIZZING SHIELD OF CAPTAIN AMERICA!

LIKE A THING ALIVE, IT ROCKETS ACROSS THE GREAT HALL, RICOCHETING BACK AT JUST THE ANGLE CAP CALCULATED...

...TO DRIVE THE UNDEAD MONSTER FROM THE AIR--

--BEFORE BOUNCING BACK TO ITS OWNER'S GRASP!

THAT ACCURSED SHIELD AGAIN!! WHEN I'M THROUGH WITH YOU, YOU'LL NEVER THROW IT OR ANYTHING ELSE AGAIN!

I DOUBT THAT!

LET ME PUT THE LIE TO HIM, CAP! THIS BLADE SHOULD WORK JUST AS WELL AS A WOODEN STAKE THROUGH THE HEART!

BARON BLOOD'S ONLY RESPONSE IS A BESTIAL SNARL, AND A SPRINGING BOUND WHICH ONCE AGAIN TAKES THE YOUTHFUL UNION JACK BY SURPRISE!

OH!

BLAZES, I WAS AFRAID OF THIS! UNION JACK IS TOO INEXPERIENCED AT THIS SORT OF THING! I HAVE TO DISTRACT THE VAMPIRE, OR JACK'S A DEAD MAN!

BARON! OVER HERE!

WITH ONE POWERFUL YANK, CAP RIPS LOOSE THE HEAVY CURTAINS, LETTING THE LATE AFTERNOON SUN FLOOD INTO THE CHAMBER!

NO!

NOT AGAIN! YOU'LL NOT BE SAVED BY THE SUN AGAIN!

LIKE A BAT OUT OF THE VERY DEPTHS OF HADES, BARON BLOOD LAUNCHES HIMSELF AT HIS STAR-SPANGLED TORMENTOR!

YOU HAVE MADE A MOST GRIEVOUS ERROR! THIS IS NOT THE LIGHT OF A RISING SUN... BUT THAT OF A SETTING ONE!

SOON IT SHALL BE TWILIGHT, AND UNTIL THEN I CAN ENDURE THE PAIN!

IN THAT CASE, I'LL JUST HAVE TO STOP YOU BEFORE SUNSET, BARON! AND BELIEVE ME, I WILL...I MUST!

I'VE PLEDGED MYSELF TO THE PRESERVATION OF LIFE AND LIBERTY...

...WHEREAS YOU REPRESENT NOTHING BUT DEATH AND DECAY! AND THAT MAKES YOU MY ENEMY, MISTER!

YES, WE ARE ENEMIES ...AND YOU ARE A FOOL! IN THE END, DEATH WINS... DEATH ALWAYS WINS!

GOT TO GET UP... AND HELP CAP, BUT... I'M SO GROGGY! BLOOD NEAR THROTTLED THE LIFE OUT OF ME!

CAP STRUGGLES VALIANTLY, BUT HE CAN FEEL BARON BLOOD'S STRENGTH SLOWLY GROWING, AS THE SUN SINKS IN THE WEST.

AND HE KNOWS, IT IS ONLY A MATTER OF TIME BEFORE THE MONSTER WINS!

IT IS THEN THAT HE RECALLS LORD FALSWORTH'S WORDS...

"THERE IS ONLY ONE WAY TO TOTALLY DESTROY A VAMPIRE!"

AND IN THAT MOMENT, HE KNOWS WHAT HE MUST DO!

NO... OH, NO.

THE DEED IS HORRIBLE TO COMPREHEND.

BUT HE KNOWS THAT HE HAS NO OTHER RECOURSE!

BLOODY--!

CHUK

AND THEN, THE CHAMPION CAN ONLY LOOK ON AS THE HUMAN FAÇADE OF BARON BLOOD MELTS AWAY, AND THE MONSTER IS REVEALED FOR WHAT HE TRULY WAS!

IT IS A VICTORY, TO BE SURE... BUT IT'S NOT A CLEAN VICTORY.

JOEY... IS IT--?

IT'S ALL OVER, KENNY. THANK HEAVEN ABOVE, IT'S OVER.

I'M JUST GLAD I WAS ABLE TO CONVINCE CAP TO LET *ME* PLAY UNION JACK. YOU'D HAVE NEVER SURVIVED HIS ATTACK.

YOU...ALWAYS WERE THE STRONGER OF US TWO, JOE.

YUH... RIGHT.

MOTHER, I DON'T KNOW IF YOU SHOULD SEE THIS!

I SAW THE WARSAW GHETTO AND THE NAZI DEATH CAMPS, KENNETH...I'LL HOLD UP. BUT, CAP--?

THE MAN'S ALL RIGHT. HE'S JUST HAD TO DO HIS JOB... AN' IT WASN'T A PLEASANT ONE. LEAVE 'IM ALONE FOR A MOMENT, OKAY?

HOURS LATER, OUT ON THE MOORS, THE LAST REMAINS OF THE UNDEAD BEAST WHICH HAD BEEN BARON BLOOD ARE CONSIGNED TO THE FLAMES--

--AND THE MENACE OF THE NAZI VAMPIRE IS ENDED FOR ALL TIME!

IT'S DONE, GRANDFATHER. BARON BLOOD WILL NEVER THREATEN ANYONE AGAIN!

DID YOU HEAR, FATHER? KENNETH SAID--!

I'M...AFRAID HE CAN'T HEAR YOU, JACKIE.

WHAT?! OH, CAP! HE...HE'S GONE! IT MUST HAVE BEEN HIS HEART. IT FINALLY GAVE OUT!

HE WAS A GOOD MAN, JACKIE...THE BEST! AND HE WENT TO HIS REWARD KNOWING THAT HIS BROTHER'S EVIL HAD BEEN OVERCOME AT LAST!

ONCE THERE WAS A MIGHTY EMPIRE, WHOSE LANDS REACHED AROUND THE GLOBE, AND UPON WHICH THE SUN NEVER SET. STRONG IT WAS, AND POWERFUL, AND NEVER DID IT MEET DEFEAT AT THE HANDS OF ANY OTHER NATION!

TIME PASSED, AND--BIT BY BIT--THE EMPIRE WAS WHITTLED AWAY, UNTIL IT WAS BUT A FRACTION OF ITS FORMER SIZE.

TODAY, THE EMPIRE IS ALL BUT GONE, AND SOME SAY THAT THE GLORY AND THE GRANDEUR OF THAT MIGHTY REALM, THAT ENGLAND, IS GONE FOREVER.

BUT THE PEOPLE OF THAT FABLED LAND LIVE ON... AND THEY ARE STILL A GOOD PEOPLE, A GREAT PEOPLE, A PEOPLE POSSESSED OF ALL THE STRENGTH, MIGHT, AND INDOMITABLE WILL WHICH FORGED THAT EMPIRE OF DAYS GONE BY.

AND AS LONG AS THAT PEOPLE ENDURES... AS LONG AS A FEW OF THOSE VALIANT HEARTS AND MINDS AND SOULS PERSIST--

--THEN SHALL THE SPIRIT OF **UNION JACK** LIVE ON!

DEDICATED TO **FRANK ROBBINS**, CREATIVE ARTIST AND STORYTELLING WIZARD... AND THE MAN WHO FIRST DREW UNION JACK...

NEXT ISSUE / WE PROUDLY CELEBRATE CAP'S 40th ANNIVERSARY WITH... The LEGEND OF CAPTAIN AMERICA!

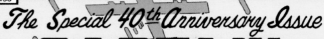

50¢

255
MAR
02453

THE MARVEL COMICS GROUP PROUDLY PRESENTS:

APPROVED
BY THE
COMICS
CODE
AUTHORITY

The Special 40th Anniversary Issue

CAPTAIN AMERICA™

COMICS

THE LIVING LEGEND!

Thrills! Chills! and More!

SEE CAP'S VERY 1ST ADVENTURE!

FM JR

JUNE, 1941... WASHINGTON, D.C.

IN THE OVAL OFFICE OF THE WHITE HOUSE, PRESIDENT FRANKLIN DELANO ROOSEVELT HAS CANCELED ALL APPOINTMENTS, FORCING CONGRESS-MEN AND V.I.P.'S ALIKE TO WAIT WHILE HE RECEIVES A VERY NON-DESCRIPT VISITOR...

...A YOUNG COURIER FROM G-2, THE INTELLIGENCE ARM OF THE DEPARTMENT OF THE ARMY.

WELL, SON, LET'S GET ON WITH IT! I HAVE THE EDITOR OF *THE WASHINGTON POST* COOL-ING HIS HEELS OUTSIDE-- AND I'M SURE I'LL HEAR ABOUT IT IN TOMORROW'S HEADLINES!

YES, SIR... I'M SORRY, SIR!

OH, THAT'S ALL RIGHT! I'VE DEVELOPED A FAIRLY THICK SKIN AS FAR AS BAD PRESS IS CONCERNED!

THIS IS IT?

YES, SIR. AS PER YOUR REQUEST, THIS IS THE FULL AND COMPLETE DOSSIER ON *OPERATION: REBIRTH!*

YOU KNOW, SON, SOMETIMES I DESPAIR. THIS WAS ONE OF THE MOST AMBITIOUS TOP-SECRET PROJECTS IN THE NATION'S HISTORY...

...AND IT CAME TO SUCH A TRAGIC END! BUT, I WANTED TO LEARN MORE ABOUT *RE-BIRTH'S* TEST SUBJECT... THIS YOUNG LAD, STEVE ROGERS, HMM... I SEE HERE--

"--THAT HE GREW UP ON THE LOWER EAST SIDE OF NEW YORK CITY! EVIDENTLY, MUCH OF HIS YOUTH WAS SPENT--

"--TRYING TO HELP HIS FAMILY MAKE ENDS MEET DURING THE DEPTHS OF THE DEPRESSION. OH... I SEE...

"...HIS FATHER DIED WHEN HE WAS STILL A CHILD, AND HIS MOTHER HAD TO STRUGGLE JUST TO KEEP HER SON AND HERSELF FED.

"STILL, DESPITE THEIR DEPRIVATION, STEVE KEPT UP WITH HIS SCHOOLING, AND BECAME A VORACIOUS READER... *ESPECIALLY OF FANTASY!*

"GIVEN THE STATE OF HIS REALITY, I CAN WELL UNDERSTAND WHY!"

"AH, IT SEEMS THAT THE BOY ALSO HAD A NATURAL TALENT FOR ART. BUT HE KEPT HIS LOVE OF ART, AND OF BOOKS, A SECRET TO AVOID TAUNTS AND BEATINGS AT THE HANDS OF HIS PEERS.

"AS THE DEPRESSION WORE ON, TIMES BECAME INCREASINGLY DIFFICULT FOR THE ROGERS' HOUSEHOLD. SARAH ROGERS TOOK IN LAUNDRY... AND TAXED HERSELF TO THE LIMIT TO PROVIDE FOR HER SON.

"BUT TIME AND HARDSHIP EVENTUALLY TOOK ITS TOLL, AND AS STEVEN ENTERED HIS LATE TEENS, HIS MOTHER PASSED ON--

"--A VICTIM OF PNEUMONIA.

"OUT ON HIS OWN, YOUNG ROGERS MANAGED TO FIND A CHEAP BOARDING HOUSE AND TOOK A JOB AS A DELIVERY BOY. IT WAS NOT AN EASY LIFE, NOR A VERY GOOD ONE...

"...BUT SOMEHOW, HE SURVIVED.

"AND THEN, ONE DAY, WHILE TRYING TO ESCAPE INTO THE FANTASY WORLD OF THE MOVIES, STEVE ROGERS ENCOUNTERED AN EVEN HARSHER REALITY--

THE SEA HAWK
ERROL FLYNN

"--IN NEWSREEL FOOTAGE OF THE NAZI WAR MACHINE IN ITS RELENTLESS MARCH ACROSS A WAR-TORN EUROPE!"

THOSE NEWSREELS... IT'S AWFUL... *AWFUL!* IT'S AS IF HALF THE WORLD HAS GONE MAD!

IF THE NAZIS AREN'T STOPPED SOON, THERE WON'T BE A FREE MAN LEFT ALIVE ANYWHERE! I HAVE TO DO SOMETHING... I *HAVE* TO!

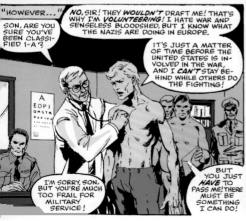

"HOWEVER..."

SON, ARE YOU SURE YOU'VE BEEN CLASSIFIED 1-A"?

NO, SIR! THEY *WOULDN'T* DRAFT ME! THAT'S WHY I'M *VOLUNTEERING!* I HATE WAR AND SENSELESS BLOODSHED, BUT I KNOW WHAT THE NAZIS ARE DOING IN EUROPE.

IT'S JUST A MATTER OF TIME BEFORE THE UNITED STATES IS INVOLVED IN THE WAR, AND I *CAN'T* STAY BEHIND WHILE OTHERS DO THE FIGHTING!

I'M SORRY, SON, BUT YOU'RE MUCH TOO FRAIL FOR MILITARY SERVICE!

BUT YOU JUST *HAVE* TO PASS ME! THERE MUST BE SOMETHING I CAN DO!

I COULDN'T HELP OVERHEARING, SON, I'M GENERAL PHILLIPS... ARE YOU REALLY SERIOUS ABOUT WANTING TO TAKE PART IN THE BIG PICTURE?

I *AM,* SIR! I'LL DO ANYTHING--*ANYTHING!*

"IT MUST HAVE BEEN KISMET! IN STEVE ROGERS, GENERAL PHILLIPS HAD FOUND THE IDEAL TEST SUBJECT FOR OPERATION: REBIRTH.

"WITHIN MINUTES, ROGERS WAS ON A PLANE, SPEEDING TOWARDS WASHINGTON. AND, AS NIGHT FELL, HE WAS TAKEN TO A SMALL CURIO SHOP ON A LITTLE-KNOWN CAPITAL SIDE STREET.

"I CAN WELL IMAGINE THE SURPRISE ROGERS FELT UPON ENTERING THAT MOLDERING OLD STOREFRONT,"

AGENTS L-7 AND X-9 REPORTING, AGENT R! THE PASSWORD IS "EAGLE."

WE HAVE "THE VISITOR" WITH US.

HALT! IDENTIFY YOURSELVES OR DIE!

ENTER AND LOCK THE DOOR BEHIND YOU!

I-I DON'T GET IT! HOW CAN SUCH AN IMPORTANT PROJECT BE HOUSED IN A SMALL SHOP LIKE THIS? NOTHING I'VE SEEN SO FAR SEEMS TO MAKE SENSE!

IN WORK SUCH AS OURS, THINGS ARE SELDOM WHAT THEY SEEM.

WHY...YOU... YOU'RE NOT--! THAT IS...I THOUGHT--!

FORGIVE THE THEATRICS. I ASSURE YOU, THEY ARE QUITE NECESSARY.

"IT MUST HAVE BEEN A NIGHT FULL OF SURPRISES FOR OUR YOUNG 'VISITOR.' AS AGENT R STOOD GUARD, ROGERS WAS CONDUCTED UP A NARROW FLIGHT OF STAIRS, THROUGH A HIDDEN DOORWAY, AND INTO ONE OF THE MOST ADVANCED BIOCHEMICAL LABORATORIES IN THE FREE WORLD,"

IT...IT'S AMAZING! LIKE SOMETHING OUT OF H.G. WELLS!

GET USED TO IT, ROGERS. YOU'RE GOING TO BE SPENDING SOME TIME HERE.

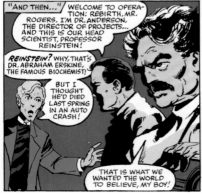

"AND THEN..." WELCOME TO OPERATION: REBIRTH, MR. ROGERS. I'M DR. ANDERSON, THE DIRECTOR OF PROJECTS... AND THIS IS OUR HEAD SCIENTIST, PROFESSOR REINSTEIN!

REINSTEIN? WHY, THAT'S DR. ABRAHAM ERSKINE, THE FAMOUS BIOCHEMIST!

BUT I THOUGHT HE'D DIED LAST SPRING IN AN AUTO CRASH!

THAT IS WHAT WE WANTED THE WORLD TO BELIEVE, MY BOY!

IT LOOKS LIKE THE SECURITY BOYS WERE RIGHT TO KEEP YOU UNDER WRAPS, ABRAHAM. YOUR FACE IS TOO RECOGNIZABLE...THE REINSTEIN CODE-NAME DIDN'T FOOL YOUNG ROGERS FOR A MINUTE!

STEVEN, WE HAVE TO LEVEL WITH YOU,... OUR EXPERIMENT MIGHT GIVE YOU A STRONG NEW BODY, BUT IT MIGHT KILL YOU!

I'M WILLING TO FACE THOSE CONSEQUENCES, SIR.

VERY WELL THEN,... WE SHALL BEGIN OUR WORK AT ONCE!

"OVER THE NEXT FEW WEEKS, ROGERS WAS PUT THROUGH A GRUELING SERIES OF TESTS TO DETERMINE THE EXACT LIMITS OF HIS PHYSICAL ABILITIES-- WHILE DR. ERSKINE WORKED ON HIS SECRET TISSUE-BUILDING SERUM!"

"AND THEN, THAT DAY ARRIVED WHEN ANDERSON BURST IN ON THE GENERAL AND MYSELF WITH THE NEWS..."

THE CHEMICAL IS PERFECTED, GENTLEMEN-- AND I SUGGEST THAT WE PROCEED AT ONCE!

THEN THE TIME HAS COME AT LAST!

THERE IS NOTHING MORE TO BE SAID. I WISH YOU ALL GOD-SPEED!

"CHANGING TO CIVILIAN CLOTHING, GENERAL PHILLIPS AND UNDER-SECRETARY SIMMS WERE CONDUCTED TO THE HIDDEN LABORATORY BY DR. ANDERSON HIMSELF."

"AND WHEN THEY ARRIVED, A MAN WHOSE CREDENTIALS IDENTIFIED HIM AS SPECIAL AGENT CLEMSON WAS ALREADY THERE..."

"...WAITING!"

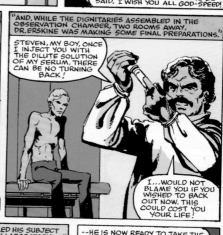

"AND, WHILE THE DIGNITARIES ASSEMBLED IN THE OBSERVATION CHAMBER, TWO ROOMS AWAY, DR. ERSKINE WAS MAKING SOME FINAL PREPARATIONS."

STEVEN, MY BOY, ONCE I INJECT YOU WITH THE DILUTE SOLUTION OF MY SERUM, THERE CAN BE NO TURNING BACK!

I...WOULD NOT BLAME YOU IF YOU WISHED TO BACK OUT NOW. THIS COULD COST YOU YOUR LIFE!

SIR, GOOD MEN FROM POLAND TO GREAT BRITAIN HAVE BEEN PUTTING THEIR LIVES ON THE LINE. CAN I DO ANY LESS?

LET'S GET ON WITH IT!

I BELIEVE YOU ARE THE BRAVEST YOUNG MAN I HAVE EVER MET!

THIS WILL STING FOR JUST A MOMENT, THEN YOU WILL FEEL A SLIGHT DIZZINESS.

"THEN, ERSKINE LED HIS SUBJECT INTO THE MAIN LABORATORY..."

GENTLEMEN, THIS DISTINGUISHED YOUNG VOLUNTEER HAS ALREADY BEEN INJECTED WITH MY SECRET SERUM--

--HE IS NOW READY TO TAKE THE ORAL FORM OF THE COMPOUND!

YOU MUST DRINK THIS QUICKLY, BEFORE THE CHEMICALS LOSE THEIR POTENCY. GOOD LUCK, MY BOY!

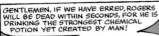

GENTLEMEN, IF WE HAVE ERRED, ROGERS WILL BE DEAD WITHIN SECONDS, FOR HE IS DRINKING THE STRONGEST CHEMICAL POTION YET CREATED BY MAN!

BUT, IF WE SUCCEED, IF HE LIVES, HE WILL BE THE FIRST OF AN ARMY OF FIGHTING MEN SUCH AS THE WORLD HAS NEVER SEEN!

HIS REFLEXES, HIS PHYSICAL CONDITION WILL BE SECOND TO NONE! AND HIS COURAGE...

...WELL HIS COURAGE HAS ALREADY BEEN PROVEN!

NOW, YOU SHALL SEE HOW I SPEED UP THE SERUM'S PROCESS-- AND HOW IT WILL AFFECT ROGERS' BODY TISSUE!

OBSERVE! I AM BOMBARDING HIS BODY WITH POTENT, INVISIBLE *VITA-RAYS!*

ONCE THE PROCESS IS COMPLETED, THE FRAIL YOUNG MAN WHO STOOD BEFORE YOU WILL BE FRAIL AND SICKLY NO LONGER!

INSTEAD, HIS EVERY BODY CELL WILL SURGE WITH NEW *POWER,* NEW *VIGOR,* NEW *VITALITY!*

YAARRGH!

E-EVERYTHING IS SPINNING AROUND! I...FEEL LIKE I'M BLACKING OUT...BUT...I...MUST...HANG ON!

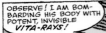

IT'S *WORKING!* DON'T GIVE UP, SON! HOLD ON! THIS IS THE MOMENT OF CRISIS! YOU *MUST* SURVIVE IT!

I...I CAN FEEL POWER SURGING THROUGH ME! MY BODY'S GETTING LARGER --*STRONGER!*

IT'S AS IF MILLIONS OF CELLS WERE FORMING AT INCREDIBLE SPEED!

IN A MATTER OF *MINUTES*-- I'VE ACTUALLY BECOME A *NEW MAN!*

"IN A MATTER OF MINUTES, THE GLEAMING HOPE OF *OPERATION: REBIRTH* CAME TO AN ABRUPT END.

"THE SECRET OF THE SUPER-SOLDIER SERUM APPARENTLY DIED WITH DR. ERSKINE, WHO HAD NEVER COMMITTED THE FULL FORMULA TO PAPER.

"AS FOR 'AGENT CLEMSON,' A MAN WE LATER IDENTIFIED AS NAZI ASSASSIN *HEINZ KRUGER*...HE, TOO, PAID THE FINAL PRICE.

"KNOCKED INTO THE VITA-RAY DEVICE'S *ELECTRICAL OMNI-VERTER* POWER SOURCE BY ROGERS' PUNCH, HE SCRAMBLED TO FREE HIMSELF--

"--AND IN DOING SO, HE GRABBED HOLD OF THE OMNI-VERTER'S HIGH-VOLTAGE TERMINALS ...AND WAS INSTANTLY ELECTROCUTED!

"THE SUPER-SOLDIER SERUM WORKED...ROGERS WAS LIVING PROOF OF THAT! BUT WE COULD NEVER PRODUCE ANOTHER MAN LIKE HIM..."

...AND SO ENDED OUR BOLD EXPERIMENT.

THE WORLD IS POORER FOR THE LOSS OF ABRAHAM ERSKINE!

YES, SIR. BUT HE DID LEAVE US AN IMPORTANT LEGACY--

--IN THE "REBORN" STEVE ROGERS. AS YOU KNOW, ACTING UPON GENERAL PHILLIPS ADVISEMENT, ROGERS BECAME THE CORNERSTONE OF...*PROJECT: SUPER-SOLDIER!*

AS *THIS* DOSSIER SHOWS, MR. PRESIDENT--

PROJECT: SUPER-SOLDIER

TOP SECRET

"--SHORTLY AFTER DR. ERSKINE'S TRAGIC DEATH, ROGERS WAS PUT INTO A SPECIAL TRAINING PROGRAM, TO TEACH HIM HOW TO BEST USE HIS NEW BODY!

"FOR THREE MONTHS, HE WORKED OUT WITH THE GREATEST BOXERS, WRESTLERS, BODY BUILDERS, AND GYMNASTS THE FREE WORLD HAD TO OFFER! AND WHATEVER TIME NOT SPENT IN PHYSICAL TRAINING WAS SPENT IN LEARNING THE FINE POINTS OF MILITARY STRATEGY AND TACTICS.

"THIS WAS PERSONALLY SUPERVISED BY GENERAL PHILLIPS!

"AND THEN, IN MARCH OF THIS YEAR..."

WELL, STEVE, I SUPPOSE YOU'VE BEEN WONDERING JUST WHAT WE'VE HAD IN MIND FOR YOU...WHAT WITH ALL OF THIS TRAINING.

I ASSUMED THAT YOU WERE GROOMING ME FOR SOME SORT OF TOP-SECRET SPECIAL MISSION, SIR.

YES, A VERY SPECIAL MISSION! YOU SEE, THE NAZIS HAVE A SPECIAL AGENT WHO IS CURRENTLY SPREADING TERROR ACROSS THE FACE OF EUROPE!

HE'S CALLED... THE RED SKULL! AND IT'S RUMORED THAT SOME MEMBERS OF THE NAZI HIGH COMMAND FEAR HIM EVEN MORE THAN THEY DO HITLER!

THE SKULL HAS COME TO PERSONIFY THE EVIL OF NAZISM. WE DESPERATELY NEED AN AGENT WHO IS HIS OPPOSITE... A MAN WHO WILL BE A LIVING SYMBOL OF LIFE AND LIBERTY!

AND... YOU WANT ME TO BE THAT MAN?

YES, STEVE...WE DO. IN THIS PACKAGE, YOU'LL FIND A UNIFORM SPECIALLY DESIGNED FOR YOU...TRY IT ON!

I...REALIZE THAT THIS IS AN AWESOME RESPONSIBILITY, STEVE. YOU'RE BEING ASKED TO REPRESENT AMERICA, TO BOTH HER PEOPLE AND THE WORLD.

BUT WE NEED YOU TO INSPIRE THE PUBLIC...TO GIVE THEM HOPE THROUGH THE DARK DAYS THAT LIE AHEAD.

THEN I PRAY THAT I'M EQUAL TO THE TASK, GENERAL! THIS LAND OF OURS MAY HAVE SEEN SOME HARD TIMES, AND MAYBE IT HASN'T ALWAYS LIVED UP TO THE PROMISE OF THE FOUNDING FATHERS...

...BUT AMERICA AT ITS BEST HAS ALWAYS STOOD FOR THE RIGHTS OF MAN, AND AGAINST THE RULE OF TYRANTS!

AND IF AMERICA NEEDS A MAN TO STAND FOR HER PRINCIPLES, TO BATTLE THE FORCES OF TYRANNY--THEN, AS GOD IS MY WITNESS, I SHALL BE THAT MAN!

"ROGERS GOT HIS FIRST CHANCE TO LIVE UP TO THAT PLEDGE JUST THREE NIGHTS LATER...WHEN, ON A DESERTED BACK ROAD IN THE MARYLAND COUNTRYSIDE--

"--AS A HIGH-RANKING COLONEL WAS BEING DRIVEN TO A TOP-SECRET MILITARY INSTALLATION ..."

BLAM
WUP-WUP-WUP-WUP

IT'S A BLOW-OUT, SIR! I'LL GET IT CHANGED AS SOON AS--HUH?!

THE ROADWAY'S BEEN COVERED WITH SOME SORT OF SPIKED BARBS!

HOLD IT RIGHT THERE, SOLDIER! ONE MOVE AND YOU WON'T LIVE TO SEE THE DAWN!

HUH?!

BAH! DO NOT WASTE YOUR TIME WITH THE ENLISTED MAN!

YES! SILENCE HIM AND SEIZE THE COLONEL--HE IS THE ONE WE WANT!

WAIT A MINUTE! YOU CAN'T-- WHUNNGH!

DO NOT TELL US WHAT WE CANNOT DO!

YOU ARE COMING WITH US, COLONEL HENSON! THE FATHERLAND WISHES TO LEARN WHAT YOU KNOW!

EH?

THAT NOISE... WHAT--?

VRRRRROOOM

YOU'RE NOT TAKING ANYONE ANYWHERE, NAZI!

MEIN GOTT!

"ROGERS' REPORT ON THAT ENCOUNTER WAS QUITE MODEST, BUT FROM THE STATEMENT WHICH WAS LATER SUBMITTED BY COLONEL HENSON--

"--IT SOUNDS LIKE OUR SUPER-SOLDIER TORE INTO THOSE FIFTH COLUMNISTS LIKE A ONE-MAN ARMY!"

SCREE-VROOM

DROP THAT TOMMY-GUN, MISTER-- DROP IT!

YOU FELLOWS DON'T LISTEN VERY WELL, DO YOU? IF YOU'RE NOT GOING TO DROP THE GUN, I'LL HAVE TO DROP YOU!

WHUNK

LOOKS LIKE THAT TIP WHICH ARMY INTELLIGENCE RECEIVED, ABOUT A POSSIBLE ATTEMPT TO KIDNAP COLONEL HENSON, WAS ON THE UP-AND-UP AFTER ALL!

FOR THE LAST SEVERAL MILES, I'D THOUGHT THIS EVENING WAS GOING TO YIELD ME NOTHING MORE THAN A NICE RIDE IN THE NIGHT AIR!

OOK

ERK

WHU

IT IS NOT POSSIBLE! THE MAN ISN'T HUMAN!

YUNNNK

THAT'S WHERE YOU'RE WRONG!

I'M TOTALLY HUMAN! BUT I'M FIGHTING FOR A CAUSE... A DREAM! AND THAT MAKES ALL THE DIFFERENCE!

VERDAMMT FOOL! WE FIGHT FOR A CAUSE, AS WELL-- THE CAUSE OF THE THIRD REICH!

YES, BUT YOUR CAUSE ISN'T A DREAM... IT'S A *NIGHTMARE!*

PTANG

PING

BUDA-BUDA

AND DON'T FLATTER YOURSELF BY THINKING THAT YOU CAN STOP ME WITH THAT CHATTER-GUN!

IT WON'T DO YOU ANY MORE GOOD THAN IT DID YOUR PARTNER!

WUMP

BUDA-BUDA-BUDA

NOW, WHERE'S THAT LEADER OF YOURS?

NO, HE MUSTN'T CAPTURE ME! I MUST GET BACK TO BUND HEADQUARTERS, AND REPORT THIS TO MY SUPERIORS!

YOU'RE NOT GOING ANYWHERE, FRITZ!

WHUU--?!

WHIZZZ

YOU'RE NOT CAUSING ANY MORE TROUBLE TONIGHT!

WHAP

EEESH!

THAT... THAT WAS THE MOST AMAZING DISPLAY OF HAND-TO-HAND COMBAT I'VE EVER SEEN!

THANK YOU, SIR, BUT I WAS JUST DOING MY JOB...KEEPING YOU AND THE NATION SAFE!

YOU CERTAINLY DO YOUR JOB VERY WELL, SON, BUT WHO IN BLAZES ARE YOU?!

WHO I AM DOESN'T MATTER, SIR... BUT YOU CAN CALL ME *CAPTAIN AMERICA!*

AND NOW, IF YOU'LL EXCUSE ME, I THINK *G-2* WILL WANT TO ASK THIS GENTLEMAN SOME QUESTIONS!

COLONEL? WHO WAS THAT MASKED MAN?

LIKE HE SAID, CORPORAL, IT DOESN'T MATTER!

"TWENTY-FOUR HOURS LATER, ALARMED BY THE FAILURE OF THEIR ATTACK SQUAD TO REPORT IN, MAJOR NAZI BUND LEADERS MET IN A SECLUDED NEW YORK WAREHOUSE--

"--WITH A RECENT ARRIVAL FROM OVERSEAS!"

THE FUEHRER WILL NOT BE PLEASED BY THIS FAILURE!

W-WE QUITE UNDERSTAND, HERR KLEIN-SCHMIDT. WE CAN'T FIGURE OUT WHAT WENT WRONG!

HOWEVER, WE HAVE HEARD RUMORS OF SOME NEW GOVERNMENT SUPER-AGENT--!

KRASH

AND HERE'S WHERE THOSE RUMORS GET CONFIRMED!

STOP HIM! HE'S ONLY ONE MAN!

YOU BUNDISTS DISGUST ME! YOU'RE NATIVE-BORN AMERICANS, MOST OF YOU...YET YOU'D SELL OUT YOUR OWN COUNTRY TO THE MOST HORRIFIC TYRANT EVER TO WALK THE EARTH!

BOP

WHAM

I'LL HOLD HIM, YOU-- UNNHHH!

KRAK

NOBODY HOLDS CAPTAIN AMERICA-- ESPECIALLY WHEN I'VE GOT MY EYES SET ON A GOAL...

...LIKE YOU, MR. NAZI AGENT!

NOBODY MOVE! THIS IS THE F.B.I.!

BLAZES, McCLOSKEY, I FIGURED WE'D HAVE A REAL BATTLE ON OUR HANDS, BUT IT LOOKS LIKE CAP'S TAKEN MOST OF THE FIGHT OUTTA THEM!

OPEN UP THE DOORS AND TELL O'BRIEN TO BRING THE WAGON AROUND!

NO, WAIT! THE HEAD BUND LEADER IS STILL RUNNING AROUND FREE!

NO GOOD! THE FEDERAL BOYS CAN'T HEAR ME...THERE'RE TOO MANY ECHOES IN THIS WAREHOUSE!

GOT TO GET TO HIM BEFORE HE CAN ESCAPE OUT THE DOUBLE DOORS!

WELL! I'M IN LUCK...IN HIS PANIC, HE RAN RIGHT PAST A POSSIBLE ESCAPE ROUTE!

I'M CALLING A HALT TO THIS BEFORE SOME INNOCENT BYSTANDER GETS HURT!

COME ON, MISTER, ALL YOU CAN DO NOW IS SURRENDER! NOTHING IN THAT PILE OF SCRAP METAL WILL HELP YOU.

YOU THINK SO, DO YOU?

WHAT'S GOING ON IN HERE?

"THE YOUNG NEWSPAPERMAN'S SHOUT MIGHT HAVE DISTRACTED ANOTHER MAN, BUT NOT CAPTAIN AMERICA! HOWEVER..."

THE MINIONS OF THE THIRD REICH SHALL NEVER FALL! THE REICH SHALL LAST A THOUSAND YEARS!

HEIL HITLER!

HE TELEGRAPHED THAT SWING BY A MILE! IT WAS EASY TO DUCK, BUT HE CAUGHT ONE OF THE WING-TIPS OF MY MASK...KNOCKED IT AJAR!

HEY! YOU WITH THE MASK...HOLD IT!

SORRY, NO TIME FOR THAT NOW!

THAT WAS CLOSE!

IT WOULDN'T DO FOR MY FACE TO BE PHOTOGRAPHED...THAT WOULD DESTROY MY EFFECTIVENESS AS AN ANONYMOUS SYMBOL! I HAVE TO GIVE SOME THOUGHT TO REDESIGNING MY MASK, SO THIS CAN'T HAPPEN AGAIN!

THIS IS THE LAST OF THEM, AGENT McCLOSKEY!

THANKS FOR THE HELP, CAP! IF WE HAD A FEW MORE AGENTS LIKE YOU, WE COULD REDUCE ESPIONAGE BY A THIRD!

"THE INFORMATION GATHERED IN THAT RAID DEALT A SEVERE BLOW TO NAZI FIFTH COLUMN ACTIVITIES, MR. PRESIDENT--"

--AND HELPED CAPTAIN AMERICA TO SHUT DOWN A NUMBER OF SPY RINGS! IT'S ALL THERE IN THE DOSSIER.

MARVELOUS! I'M GRATIFIED TO SEE THAT THE ACTIVITIES OF OUR CAPTAIN HAVE BEEN SO WELL DOCUMENTED. THIS ENTRY, FOR EXAMPLE--

"--DEALING WITH THE ATTEMPTED THEFT OF A NEW BOMB-SIGHT FROM THE GRUMMAN AIRCRAFT PLANT!

"THREE AXIS AGENTS HAD GAINED ENTRY, DISGUISED AS ARMED FORCES PERSONNEL.

"BUT..."

YOU MIGHT HAVE FOOLED THOSE GUARDS AT THE GATE, BUT YOU DIDN'T FOOL ME, 'MAJOR'.

EVEN IF I HADN'T BEEN TAILING YOUR LITTLE CREW FOR THESE PAST THREE HOURS...THOSE SHOES YOU'RE WEARING WOULD HAVE BEEN A DEAD GIVEAWAY!

THEY'RE HARDLY REGULATION FOOTWEAR!

ACH!

AND AS FOR THESE PHONY 'AIDES' OF YOURS--!

BAM

WUD

"IN LESS THAN A MINUTE, CAPTAIN AMERICA HAD ENDED ALL ENEMY RESISTANCE AND DISAPPEARED INTO THE NIGHT, LEAVING THREE BEDRAGGLED SPIES BEHIND FOR THE MILITARY POLICE TO CART AWAY.

"TWO WEEKS LATER, AT ANOTHER IMPORTANT INSTALLATION..."

LIBERTY SHIP-YARDS

QUICKLY... BEFORE ANYONE SEES YOU!

DO NOT WORRY, MY FRIEND, BY THE TIME ANYONE IS AROUND TO SEE ANYTHING, IT WILL BE TOO LATE!

VERY WELL... IN HERE! HURRY!

"SECONDS LATER..."

THERE, THE EXPLOSIVE CHARGE IS IN PLACE! WHEN THE ASSEMBLY LINES START TO RUN TOMORROW, THIS ENTIRE FACTORY WILL BE LEVELED!

AH... AH...AH...

YES? WHAT IS IT?

"AND FINALLY, JUST LAST WEEK, FOLLOWING INFORMATION GATHERED BY THE F.B.I. AND G-2, CAPTAIN AMERICA STOPPED ONE OF THE MOST INCREDIBLE PLOTS EVER SET IN MOTION AGAINST THIS NATION IN PEACETIME--

"--THE ATTEMPTED DESTRUCTION OF *BOULDER DAM!*"

"DISGUISED AS MAINTENANCE MEN, THREE SABOTEURS WERE CAUGHT RED-HANDED, SETTING HIGH-EXPLOSIVE CHARGES IN THE MIGHTY TURBINE GENERATORS OF THE DAM'S HYDRO-ELECTRIC PLANT!

"AGAINST AMERICA'S SUPER-SOLDIER--

"--THEY NEVER HAD A CHANCE!

WAMM

"WERE IT NOT FOR CAPTAIN AMERICA, THIS NATION WOULD HAVE LOST AN IMPORTANT SOURCE OF WATER AND ELECTRICAL POWER. WE OWE THAT MAN A GREAT DEAL--"

--AND I HAVE LITTLE DOUBT THAT, BEFORE THE INTERNATIONAL AFFAIRS OF MAN ARE ONCE AGAIN PUT IN ORDER, WE WILL BE EVEN MORE IN HIS DEBT!

WELL, WHEN DO I GET TO MEET OUR SUPER-SOLDIER?

RIGHT AWAY, SIR!

CAPTAIN--!

THE DOOR TO THE OVAL OFFICE SWINGS WIDE, AND...

GOOD MORNING, MR. PRESIDENT. THIS IS A GREAT HONOR!

YOUR FIRE-SIDE CHATS ON THE RADIO HAVE BEEN AN INSPIRATION TO US ALL.

THANK YOU, SON, BUT I DARE SAY I'M NOT THE ONLY ONE PRESENT IN THIS OFFICE WHO'S BEEN AN INSPIRATION.

AS A MATTER OF FACT, I'VE READ MORE ABOUT YOU IN THE PAPERS LATELY, THAN I HAVE ABOUT ME!

GOOD THING THIS ISN'T AN ELECTION YEAR, EH?

I SEE THAT ARMY ORDNANCE HAS FINALLY MADE THE ALTERATIONS IN YOUR UNIFORM.

YES, SIR, MR. PRESIDENT. I WON'T HAVE TO WORRY ABOUT LOSING MY MASK IN BATTLE ANY LONGER... AND THE ADDED DURALUMIN CHAIN-MAIL PROVIDES EXCELLENT PROTECTION FOR MY NECK!

YES, WELL, I HAVE ANOTHER LITTLE ADDITION FOR YOUR BATTLE GEAR.

A NEW SHIELD! IT'S...MAGNIFICENT! IT'S MUCH LIGHTER THAN MY OLD SHIELD, AND WITH ITS DISCUS-LIKE SHAPE, I'LL BE ABLE TO HURL IT TWICE AS FAR!

IT SHOULD BE AS EFFECTIVE AN OFFENSIVE WEAPON AS A DEFENSIVE ONE! I ASSUME IT'S AS BULLETPROOF AS MY OLD SHIELD?

EVEN MORE SO! IN FACT, I'M TOLD THAT THE METAL IN THE SHIELD HAS SOME INCREDIBLE PROPERTIES.

IF ONLY THE METALUR-GICAL ACCIDENT WHICH PRODUCED IT COULD BE DUPLICATED...

AH, BUT THIS IS NO TIME FOR RE-CRIMINATIONS! CAPTAIN, ARE YOU READY FOR THE SECOND PHASE OF PROJECT: SUPER-SOLDIER?

SIR, I'M READY FOR ANYTHING.

SPLENDID! THE ARMY HAS DEVISED A PLAN TO ENABLE YOU TO MOVE ABOUT IN SECRET, BUT STILL BE CLOSE BY FOR SPECIAL MISSIONS. WE'RE GOING TO GIVE YOU A COVER IDENTITY...

JULY, 1941... CAMP LEHIGH.

STEVE ROGERS...NOW *PRIVATE* STEVE ROGERS...ADJUSTS TO THE ROUTINE OF ARMY BOOT CAMP...

ROGERS, YOU MEATHEAD, IS THAT THE *ONLY* POSITION YOU KNOW?

NO, SIR. WHAT POSITION DO YOU WANT?

NO TALKING AT ATTENTION! *I* DO THE TALKING! NOW...

...PARAAADE REST!

OWWW! NOT ON MY FOOT, YOU @!xx!@!x IDJIT!

UH-OH.

@xx☆!!©xx! WHY? WHY, OF ALL THE SERGEANTS IN THIS MAN'S ARMY, DID I GET STUCK WITH A FUMBLE-BUTT LIKE YOU?!

GEE, I DON'T KNOW, SARGE. I...

ROGERS

SHADDAP!

JUST THEN...

HEY, SARGE! COLONEL FEENEY WANTS TO SEE YA OVER AT H.Q.

YEAH? THANKS, BARNES!

YOU GET OFF LUCKY THIS TIME, ROGERS!

DIS-MISSED!

SGT. DUFFY IS REALLY AN ALL-RIGHT JOE. I HATE TO GIVE HIM A HARD TIME, BUT THE PENTAGON WANTS ME TO PLAY THE CLUMSY RECRUIT... SO NO ONE WILL SUSPECT ME OF BEING CAPTAIN AMERICA.

I'D STAY OUTTA HIS WAY FOR A WHILE, STEVE! HE'S GONNA BE EVEN MADDER WHEN HE FINDS OUT THERE AIN'T NO COLONEL FEENEY!

WHAT? THERE ISN'T?

NAW! I JUST FIGURED YOU COULD USE A BREATHER FROM THAT CHEWIN' OUT, AND HE WON'T PICK ON ME! HECK, EVER SINCE MY OLD MAN DIED IN BASIC TRAINING, AND I WAS ADOPTED AS CAMP MASCOT, I CAN GET AWAY WITH JUST ABOUT ANYTHING!

WELL, I APPRECIATE THE FAVOR, BUCKY. C'MON, AND I'LL BUY YOU A COKE AT THE P.X.

GEE, THANKS, STEVE! SAY, DIDJA READ THE LATEST ABOUT CAPTAIN AMERICA?

NO. WHAT'S HE UP TO NOW?

2ND INF BN

HE BROKE UP ANOTHER NEST OF NAZI SPIES! BOY, WOULDN'T IT BE GREAT TO HAVE A GUY LIKE HIM AROUND?

AW, WHO NEEDS 'IM, BUCK? YOU'VE GOT ME, HAVEN'T YOU?

WOTTA GUY! YOU'RE ALWAYS CLOWNIN', STEVE!

POST-COURIER

CAPTAIN AMERICA NABS SPY RING

BUT ONE NIGHT, JUST A FEW MONTHS LATER, YOUNG JAMES BUCHANAN BARNES STUMBLED ACROSS ONE OF HIS NATION'S MOST GUARDED SECRETS, AND CHANGED HIS LIFE FOR ALL TIME!

PLEDGING TO KEEP STEVE'S SECRET, BUCKY UNDER-WENT MONTHS OF INTENSIVE TRAINING, BECOMING CAP'S PARTNER IN THE WAR AGAINST TYRANNY!

THEN CAME THAT AWFUL DAY... *DECEMBER 7th, 1941.* AND AMERICA WAS TRULY AT WAR!

BEFORE THE YEAR HAD ENDED, CAP AND BUCKY FOUND THEMSELVES ALLIED WITH A GROUP OF POWERFUL BEINGS...A SUPER-TEAM WHICH WINSTON CHURCHILL DUBBED *THE INVADERS!*

FOR FOUR INCREDIBLE YEARS, THEY BATTLED THE NAZI MENACE--

--IN ALL OF ITS BIZARRE FORMS!

THEN, IN THE WAR'S FINAL DAYS, TRAGEDY STRUCK AGAIN! WHILE TRYING TO STOP A RUNAWAY, EXPERIMENTAL DRONE PLANE, CAP AND BUCKY WERE CAUGHT ON THE SPEEDING CRAFT AS IT HEADED OUT OVER THE NORTH ATLANTIC.

SUDDENLY, THE PLANE EXPLODED! BUCKY WAS KILLED INSTANTLY, BUT CAP WAS THROWN CLEAR OF THE EXPLOSION, PLUNGING INTO ICY ARCTIC WATERS.

THERE, THROUGH A FREAK ACCIDENT, HE WAS FROZEN INTO A STATE OF SUSPENDED ANIMATION. DECADES PASSED...

...AND FINALLY, CAP'S BODY WAS FOUND BY A NEW SUPER-TEAM WHICH HAD COME INTO BEING... A TEAM CALLED *THE AVENGERS!*

THEY VIEWED THEIR FIND WITH AWE, FOR MANY OF THE AVENGERS HAD FOUND INSPIRATION IN THE HISTORY-MAKING EXPLOITS OF THIS RED-WHITE-AND-BLUE LEGEND!

AND THEY WERE EVEN MORE AWED TO DISCOVER THAT CAP WAS NOT DEAD! THE LEGEND LIVED! AND HE SOON TOOK HIS PLACE AMONG THEM, OFTTIMES AS LEADER!

BUT STILL, EVEN AS AN AVENGER, HE WAS A MAN DECADES OUT OF TIME. AND IN THE MONTHS THAT FOLLOWED, STEVE ROGERS STROVE TO FIND A PLACE FOR HIMSELF IN THIS BRAVE NEW WORLD.

HE STROVE... AND SEARCHED... AND SUCCEEDED.

TODAY. THE SKIES ARE STILL DARK, AND DAWN IS MANY HOURS AWAY FOR NEW YORK CITY.

HERE, IN THIS APART-MENT HOUSE AT 569 LEAMAN PLACE, IN BROOKLYN HEIGHTS, ALL IS SILENT...

...AS A FOURTH FLOOR WINDOW IS SUDDENLY OPENED FROM THE OUTSIDE BY A RED-GAUNTLETED HAND.

CAPTAIN AMERICA HAS COME HOME!

WHAT A DAY! AM I BEAT!

I COULD REALLY USE A FULL NIGHT'S SLEEP, BUT AS STEVE ROGERS, I HAVE A SET OF AD STORYBOARDS TO FINISH BY MORNING.

DEADLINES ARE THE BANE OF A FREELANCE ARTIST'S LIFE. BUT...AW, I HAVE TO GET THE WORK DONE. I GAVE MY WORD I'D TURN IT IN ON TIME!

I'LL JUST TURN ON THE TUBE FOR A LITTLE BACKGROUND NOISE...

...AND HERE ARE THE FINAL NEWS HEAD-LINES. TROUBLE CONTINUES IN THE MIDEAST AT THIS HOUR...THE WALL STREET INDEX WAS OFF ANOTHER FIVE POINTS TODAY...

LET'S SEE, WHERE DO I START?

BOY, IT'S SO HARD AT TIMES, LIVING TWO LIVES, AND I'M SO TIRED....IS IT REALLY WORTH IT?

...AND FIVE THOUSAND LIVES WERE SAVED TONIGHT WHEN CAPTAIN AMERICA AVERTED A PANIC AT MADISON SQUARE GARDEN! THIS NOW COMPLETE OUR BROADCAST DAY.

O-OH! SAY, CAN YOU SEE, BY THE DAWN'S EARLY LIGHT, WHAT SO PROUD-LY WE HAILED AT THE TWILIGHT'S LAST GLEAMING? WHOSE BROAD STRIPES AND BRIGHT STARS, THRO' THE PERILOUS FIGHT--

--O'ER THE RAMPARTS WE WATCHED WERE SO GALLANTLY STREAMING? AND THE ROCKET'S RED GLARE, THE BOMBS BURSTING IN AIR, GAVE PROOF THRO' THE NIGHT THAT OUR FLAG WAS STILL THERE.

OH! SAY, DOES THAT STAR-SPANGLED BAN-NER YET WAVE O'ER THE LAND OF THE FREE..., AND THE HOME OF THE BRAVE!

IT'S WORTH IT.

AND THE LEGEND STILL LIVES ON...

...AND THE DREAM NEVER ENDS!